Near Horizons

Near Horizons

A Weekender's Guide to
Easy Trips from Albuquerque

M.J. Cain

Illustrations by Cirrelda Snider

Cirrelda Snider
July 2003

La Alameda Press   Albuquerque

La Alameda Press
9636 Guadalupe Trail NW
Albuquerque, New Mexico 87114

Contents

for ol' David
"in for a dime, in for a dollar"

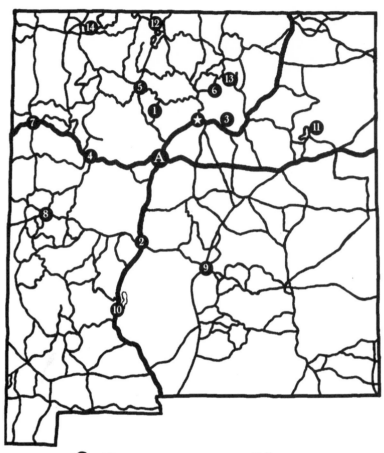

A	Albuquerque	7	Gallup
✪	Santa Fe	8	Quemado
1	Jemez Springs	9	Carrizozo / Capitan
2	Socorro	10	Truth or Consequences
3	Pecos	11	Conchas Lake
4	Grants	12	Dulce / Chama
5	Cuba	13	Tres Ritos
6	Chimayó	14	Aztec

Introduction

This is a guidebook designed to assist the Albuquerque dweller who may not have a lot of time, or a huge budget, but who still needs regular doses of "escape." Santa Fe and Taos are not discussed, because so many tour books cover these famous towns so well. Other choices like Silver City or Raton are one gas stop beyond a real fast outing. Yet there are a host of places roughly 1 to 3.5 hours away just fine for a weekend, if not necessarily ideal for a long vacation. Trips are chosen based on distances that are an easy reach from Albuquerque (primary destinations are 179 miles or less). Beware that New Mexico's little communities do not possess the glamour, or the pretensions, of say, Telluride. The weekend traveler should be prepared for some trade-offs. You will probably not bump into Tom Cruise (who got married in Telluride). But these pin dots on the map are quicker to get to, and prices tend to be lower locally than in other areas of the Southwest, though there are exceptions, particularly near Santa Fe. Modest motels will sometimes accept your pet, which the swanky resorts frown on. Price approximations refer to double occupancy. Also, because New Mexico has such a limited population, many national forests here are not crowded, unlike California or Colorado, except for major holidays.

As I traveled around the state, however, I often found it tough to obtain the information that I required on these areas. Since available accommodations may not be up to AAA standards, many facilities are *not* listed in the standard guidebooks. Some of the motels or lodges (from humble to fancy), on the other hand, aren't bad places to stay, but they don't advertise heavily. The town of Grants, an interstate exit, may receive semi-decent coverage. Yet if you plan on spending a weekend in underreported Carrizozo, adjacent to a nifty state park preserving a twisted sea of lava, you will probably wish to know if there is anywhere to spend the night. There is. A few books provide general, even exhaustive, info on attractions or background or routing possibilities, but without sufficient insight into amenities. Others prioritize the practicalities, but fail to give you the feel of the area. A guidebook describing the whole state cannot flesh out a more selective region quite as thoroughly. Newcomers need hints on various seasonal nuances, like the advantageous times to catch the birds at Bosque del Apache, and not just when it's open.

Long-term residents may want details or options that they have never explored, or updates on extremely well-known favorites that are changing. The proliferation of " B and B's" over the last ten to fifteen years has made several tiny communities much more accessible. In short, Albuquerque is actually pretty well situated, *if* you like the outdoors. Or if you are willing to drive your car onto a couple of unpaved but negotiable roads. And, unlike much of the United States, Native Americans here are a significant part of the cultural landscape. Some 19 pueblos still exist, plus big Navajo and Apache reservations. Moreover, Albuquerque sits near an amazing number of national monuments, public lands, and geological wonders such as old volcanoes. In fact, volcanic activity sculpted a staggering portion of the region.

Additionally, people who grew up here, or who have adapted, understand the advantages of multiple environments. It takes a while for the new resident to figure this out. For example, the high mountain country is most desirable during the summer and early autumn, when the city swelters (skiers prefer the mountains in the winter, naturally). In the hot months, gorgeous wild flowers bloom along the meadows and trails at upper elevations. The temperature at 9500 feet might be in the 70s, perfect for a hike or picnic. (You still need a sweater when it rains in the afternoon this far up, so be careful; the summer "monsoons" carry precipitation from as far away as the Gulf of Mexico into the Southwest.) Fall touches the mountain aspens first, turning them to glitter, before reaching the cottonwoods lower down in the Rio Grande valley. But mountain roads are often treacherous, or closed, in winter. The snow pack high up may not surrender until May (absolutely *critical* for hikers). The desert can be at its best during the winter or early spring, when it is usually a little warmer and more comfortable than Albuquerque. Obviously, the Chihuahua Desert, which dominates the southern portion of the state, can also be an inferno in July.

The winds in New Mexico are typically fierce in March or somewhat later. Snowstorms occasionally hit the plateau country even in April. Yet the plains to the east, and Colorado Plateau to the west/northwest, may be espe-

Enjoy a lunch in beautiful "somewhere else"

cially pleasant during the "transition seasons," when certain plants begin to regain, or lose, their warm season color. Chaco Canyon in autumn is wonderful. The vast steppe of the Great Plains is slashed by green in late spring, and it's still possible to find pronghorns roaming this landscape. In other words, each season offers distinct possibilities when there's so much topographic variation.

Here are a few more thoughts. This book contains suggestions for day hikes to motivate the average person in decent shape to explore. It is not specifically intended for the determined backpacker or RV camper *per se*, though there are *innumerable* solid tips on camping opportunities. (*Always* lock your car and hide your valuables when out hiking, and bring a canteen of water). There are some excellent sources (books, magazines, government brochures) that supply much more thorough data on trails, RV camping facilities, ghost towns, etc. Nevertheless, insights are tucked in that cater to a very wide scope of interests. Many phone numbers are provided for relevant services or agencies. Be advised that changes occur constantly; a given dirt road might be freshly paved, or rutted after a rainstorm, by the time you make your trip. Remember that unpaved roads are manageable when dry, even in a sedan, but can become quagmires after severe weather. The reader would do well to obtain a *Recreation Map of New Mexico* or a *New Mexico Road and Recreation Atlas* (check drugstores, bookstores, and AAA). Note that the standard AAA map may not show the smallest locations, like Tres Ritos.

Also, since many of the towns included are of minimal size, they may not have the best restaurants or supermarkets. These are places where the countryside, and the local hog contest, are more important. Quite a few eateries are mentioned, but people with well-defined requirements should shop at their preferred grocery store or deli in Albuquerque, in order to stock up the old ice chest. My spouse will not venture anywhere without a coffee maker. Tourist cabins often have their own frig/stove set-up. By the way, *definitely* mention your AAA card, AARP card, or whatever, at the chain motels to get discounts, since these places sometimes really hike their rates in summer.

For the vista-starved Duke City denizen, here are some close getaways to help you scratch the itch.

Jemez Springs

Population: 600
Elevation: 6306 ft.
Distance from Albuquerque: 56 miles
Jemez Village Office: 829-3540

A few farms tucked between tall crimson cliffs, plenteous cottonwoods specked with fishing spots, and Indian frybread stands, all greet you on the way to Jemez Springs, once you get off recently repaved Hwy. 550 (old Hwy. 44 from Bernalillo). The sign for the Perea Nature Trail appears only a short distance before the turn onto NM 4. You will take a right at San Ysidro (so designated for the patron saint of farmers), a Spanish community with colonial roots, a restored church, a Chinese café, a burger stand, and, thankfully, a gas station. You can make a comfort stop at the La Junta picnic area, several miles to the south of Jemez Springs. The Bluffs fishing access materializes a little later, and it contains a genial walk among riverside groves that are transformed each autumn into a wondrous shade of coppery gold. In spring, plum, pear, and apple saplings explode with chubby pink or white flowers as the deciduous trees stealthily reawaken.

The Jemez Mountains, now covered with dense conifer forests, are largely of volcanic origin. Water and wind carved out the narrow canyon composed of compacted volcanic ash and sandstone. The region is bountiful enough to have been inhabited off and on for ten thousand years. Prehistoric Indians collected sleek, glassy obsidian and chalcedony for making stone tools, and much later, one of Coronado's captains evidently stopped here briefly to obtain sulfur during the early 1540s. Don Juan de Oñate, New Mexico's premier colonizer, visited local pueblos at the turn of the seventeenth century, marking them for Christianizing influences.

General

Jemez Springs was named for the Jemez (or Xemez) Indians and for the warm waters enjoyed here over many centuries. Some tens of thousands of indigenous people lived in the Jemez Valley at the time of initial European contact during the 1500s. There were seven to nine separate enclaves of native residents, which had coalesced over a period of three hundred years. The area speedily evolved into a bustling mission site within the opening decades of the 1600s. It supported two churches that ministered among as many villages. Occupants were pulled in, perhaps reluctantly, from the surrounding mesa settlements to the river communities, as Franciscan proselytizing efforts gathered fiery momentum. At that time, the bubbling springs were utilized by the Spaniards and loosely identified with the fancy St. Joseph's Mission at Giusewa. San Diego Mission at Walatowa village was founded second. European plagues, however, and then rebellion, drastically winnowed and scattered the valley inhabitants.

By the first ten years of the eighteenth century, San Diego, rebuilt several times, served a diminishing native hamlet of 300. A couple of thriving Hispano ranches were noted in the vicinity by roving friars during the mid-1700s. The settlers and Amerindians grew corn, cotton, and wheat. Called Hot Springs by the first half of the nineteenth century, the locale survived phases as a farming center, raucous range-war zone, and dissolute gambling den, influenced by the discovery of a nearby gold pocket in 1889. In the meantime, the town's resort status blossomed when one of the springs erupted into a geyser around 1860. The bathhouse was built ten years later. The place carried the surname of the Archuleta family from the very late 1800s until 1907, the time that Jemez Springs as such was born.

Today, Jemez Springs is a haven for two Zen centers as well as a couple of galleries, and was deemed the smallest All-American City in 1995 (whatever that means) in part because of a beautification and clean-up drive. NM 4 was declared a National Scenic Byway in 1998, one of 55 such routes in the United States. Everyone in Santa Fe and Albuquerque knows about Jemez Springs, but info on accommodations can be spotty. Several slightly pricey but quiet mom and pop lodgings (many restricted to non-smoking adults) have developed to appeal to a variety of tastes, although you will probably want to bring some supplies along, as restaurants per se are limited. July 4 can be busy because of a parade and fireworks display. A moderate amount of growth has occurred in the valley over the last few years, as in much of Sandoval County. The designation of certain tracts as public wilderness forms a topic of considerable local discussion. If you go past the north end of town, unpaved access routes loop up into the steep slopes of higher elevations, showcasing summer homes. Virgin and Cat Mesas surround the immediate area of the village.

Practicalities

The Los Ojos Café (open daily) shows up on the right side of the highway if you are coming from Albuquerque. The name is an indirect reference to the springs, since *ojo* (or, eye in Spanish) alludes figuratively to an opening in the earth. In operation for many years, Los Ojos exudes a dark, funky saloon atmosphere memorable for its animal heads on the walls, big fireplace, pool tables, pressed tin ceilings, and pretty good New Mexican plates, burgers, and choices in beer. A tiny patio opens upstairs in the summer. Bands play here on Saturday nights. Check out the jukebox if you like the Chiffons. Consetta's Restaurant (16351 Hwy. 4) is a second option with Italian specialties located just south of the village, open 5-9:30 pm for dinner. Consetta's often serves lunch during the busy season. Deb's Highway Delights (17607 Hwy. 4) whisks up breakfast, lunch, and tasty snacks across from Los Ojos Café, and at this writing, Deb's fixes a morning buffet on Sundays. Piccadilly Pizza is tucked in a convenience store 10 miles south of town, where one can also pick up fried chicken, donuts, etc. You'll find a small country store at the south end of town.

Jemez Springs tends to buzz more during the warmer months, after the snows melt in the adjacent mountains. Several lodgings are tethered close to Hwy. 4, as you go down short country lanes that lead to the river's edge. The Dancing Bear B and B ($75-125 range; 829-3336; 314 San Diego Loop) is almost 3 miles south of the village, or 15 miles from Hwy. 550. The rates vary by room. The large suite opening onto a deck is the most expensive, and it has a frig/coffee pot; all rooms contain televisions and VCRs. Breakfast includes French toast and other delights. The living room has cathedral windows, and even a fireplace, as do some of the guestrooms (no smoking). The Desert Willow Bed and Breakfast ($100-110 range; 829-3410; 15973 Hwy.

4) overlooks a garden and the river. Watch for the sign along the highway, 16 miles from where you leave 550 at San Ysidro. The River Dancer, a nice B and B, also lies south of town ($85-160; 829-3262; 16445 Hwy. 4). This place offers a better deal during winter. The Giggling Star ($90-135 range; 829-9179; 40 Abousleman Loop; no kids or pets) is a quiet refuge of three cute cabins with fireplaces and kitchenettes on the river, opposite the Laughing Lizard; look for the small sign. The Jemez Mountain Inn ($70-95 range; 829-3926; 16445 Hwy. 4; no kids/pets) likewise keeps rooms with kitchenettes and cable TV. The inn is situated on the left (west) across from a church as you drive up to Los Ojos Café. The six suites open onto a patio or deck. The Jemez Canyon Inn ($40-60 range; 829-3254; 50 Canyon Court Rd.) hangs just off Hwy. 4 to the left as you approach from Albuquerque, after a turn at the Wolf Moon Gallery. The cabins face a field with a long shed between the stream and the main drag, and the clean, unpretentious little suites are provided with a microwave, mini-frig, plates, and silverware. There's also a loft, and whole families are ok. The Laughing Lizard Motel ($55-70 range; 829-3108) is easy to identify on the east side of the highway inside the village. The motel operates a café on the weekends during spring-summer season. The adobe Casa Blanca B and B ($100 range; 829-3579), across from the Laughing Lizard, has kitchenettes available and proffers slightly lower rates for a full week's booking. To the north at the even-teenier speck of La Cueva, the La Cueva Lodge (829-3300) sits at the intersection of Hwy. 4 and Road 126, and there's a handy convenience store next to a sometimes-open restaurant in front. A public picnic area crops up on the other side of the highway. The romantic Elk Mountain Lodge ($80-160 range; 829-3159), with its various rooms and cabin (four have whirlpool tubs plus rustic paneling), straddles the enveloping woods .5 mile up Road 126.

Things to do

Jemez Pueblo (834-7235; elevation 5479 ft.; no photos) endures 12 miles back down Hwy. 4. Today's hamlet of 3,400 is thought to be the last remaining Towa-speaking community in New Mexico. Towa is a subcategory of Tanoan, one of five major linguistic classifications for Southwest Indians. The village hedges mostly along the west side of the road. San Diego Mission Church celebrates a fall feast day with lively corn dances and aromatic food stalls at the plaza on November 12, while the feast of St. Persingula is likewise open to the public on August 2. After the Pueblo Revolt, the Spanish king issued a land grant to these people, as well as to the other surviving native towns. Even now, episodic legal hearings struggle to divvy up limited water resources between the Jemez Indians and the other residents of the Jemez Valley. Travelers may not walk around the pueblo at will, but you can risk a very quick drive-through. The newish, attractive Walatowa Visitor's Center, at the Jemez Red Rocks a couple of miles north of the pueblo, is open from about 10-4 daily (longer hours in summer), and it encompasses a photo exhibit, a gift shop with Jemez pottery, and a nature walk. Ask about the CDs featuring either the Black Eagle or Star Feather Powwow Singers, interrelated Jemez Pueblo outfits nominated for a Grammy in 2002. You can buy gas at the adjacent convenience store. Note that there are no gas stations in Jemez Springs. Located right on Hwy. 4, the Visitor's Center, aided in part by the Forest Service, offers information on other pueblos throughout the state. It's the first all-tribe facility of this type in New Mexico. The Memorial Day weekend is a good time to come if you want to enjoy the Jemez Annual Crafts Fair, a fiesta of 100 booths and all-day dances. A Winter Crafts Show takes place the first weekend in December. One should also be able to catch serious ritual dancing here on Virgin of Guadalupe Day (December 12), Christmas Day, New Year's Day, and Three King's Day (January 6); festivities often start rolling as early as 8 or 9 am, but schedules may change, so *call* for times.

Sipping the nectar of the Ponderosa Vineyard (834-7487; 3171 Rte. 290; open Tues.-Sat. 10-5; 12-5 on Sun.) makes for an easy side trip. From Jemez Pueblo, find the road headed east (Rte. 290). Juicy grapes are grown at an elevation of 5800 ft. in the volcanic ash of the Ponderosa Valley to make award-wining selections of wine. This vineyard is considered to be the largest producer of Riesling in the state. A bar and grill of sorts abides in Ponderosa, as well as a couple of 1957 Chevys. If one keeps going through the "suburb" of Vallecitos, the pavement will run out in about four miles, as you meander through the appealing valley of Vallecitos Creek beneath rust-colored cliffs. Then Forest Road 10 begins. The Paliza Group Campground should become visible in 1 and .5 miles; continue for another .5 mile to the main Paliza Campground, just to the right at the fork by the bridge. This nook is a handsome swatch of forest in the south Jemez Mts., and enormous Ponderosa pines shelter the campsites, a very convenient outdoor escape from Albuquerque (fee: $8). There are covered picnic tables and a wispy streamlet that runs in early summer. For some hair-raising diversion, explore Forest Road 266, a coiling, hillside drive affording a great vista of the Paliza and San Juan Canyons.

Gilman Tunnels are worth a peek. Just north of Cañon, veer left (northwest) from Hwy. 4 through Cañones onto Route 485, and proceed for some five miles. These unusual man-made hollows were blasted from the surrounding rock to accommodate a logging train during the 1920s. The road narrows as it writhes into a deep canyon, and an overlook provides an invigorating view of the Rio Guadalupe. These waters churn and crash after the winter snowmelt. Once or twice unwary hikers have scampered over the slippery rocks possessed by a manic desire to wade here, and then had to be rescued hours later drenching wet and cold. Resign yourself to taking photographs. Often open during warm weather, F.R. 376 may be pursued for the next 15 or so miles, becoming dirt as it maneuvers over Schoolhouse Mesa, echoing the creek and then arching to the right (east), before exiting onto Road 126 at a point 5 miles from Fenton Lake.

There are other options not to be forgotten. What do you do in a place with hot springs? Well, you can soak, humidify, and detoxify. The Jemez Bath House (829-3303) harkens to the 1870s with renovations from the 1940s. This facility, on the west side of NM 4 a few steps from Los Ojos, has concrete tubs in the women's wing, and another four in the men's wing. You might need to make reservations during a hectic weekend, but facials ($45), pedicures, and manicures are available. A private soak runs $9 for 30 minutes or $12 for 60 minutes, while massages cost from $30-69. Summer hours are from 9 am-9 pm, and 10 am-7:30 pm during the rest of the year. The water temperature sizzles at 154-176 degrees.

The Jemez State Monument (open daily 8:30 am-5 pm except December 25, January 1, Easter, and Thanksgiving; $3 fee; 829-3530), in operation since 1970, is .5 mile north of Jemez Springs on the east side of Hwy. 4. It embraces the ruins of Giusewa (translated as boiling waters), a precursor of today's Jemez Pueblo, built some 600 years ago, and once two stories in height. A little trail enables one to ramble among the

Jemez Canyon / Cañon de San Diego

chunky wall portions of San José de los Jemez Church (ca. 1621-1626), which had a nave 110 feet long. While New Mexico still retains a handful of its seventeenth-century churches, structures (even collapsed ones) from the first quarter of the 1600s are few and important. This one was founded by the zealous and formidable Fray Geronimo Salmerón, a key leader of the Franciscans. The mission was possibly damaged by a fire (at least it seems to have been deserted after fifteen years) and deteriorated further during the Pueblo Revolt of 1680. Hispanic Culture Day is celebrated sometime between June 30 and July 9, whereas a luminaria tour lights up for one enchanted night each year during mid-December.

Soda Dam lies 1.5 miles from the village up Hwy. 4. This natural formation is an interesting 50 foot-high, 300 foot-long arm of calcium carbonate, the deposit of a spring that has pinched the Jemez River into a waterfall and series of pools. The spring occasionally emits a strange noxious odor because of its sulfurous content. You can revive your tired feet in the tumbling waters, though this spot may be crowded in summer. From the upper car turnout, look for the walk to the top of the rock mound for a visual sweep of the river. From the first or lower turnout, tiny Jemez Cave nestles a hundred feet up the spillway, an archeological site that once contained artifacts such as spear throwers (called atlatls) and sandals, not to mention the mummified remains of a child dated to 1250 AD.

The Handmaids of the Precious Blood in the Cor Jesu Monastery and Fitzgerald-Via Coeli Monastery are two of the ever-curious roadway sights in Jemez Springs. Both groups were organized in 1947. The Handmaids were established as a contemplative order by the Archdiocese to pray for troubled priests in spiritual need. Via Coeli, which means heavenly way, houses the Servants of the Holy Paraclete (the Holy Spirit). Father G. Fitzgerald began this manicured, priestly retreat, embellished with restful gardens and art objects, and tours or special functions can be arranged through the staff now and again. The Hummingbird Music Camp north of town is another spread in this area with a winding stream that hosts periodic meditation classes, art shows, etc. (check the bimonthly local newspaper).

Battleship Rock, a 200' vertical prow of welded volcanic tuff, juts out majestically maybe five miles north of the village on NM 4. The Forest Service has recently improved picnic and camping facilities here (fees start at $4). Right before you pass the massive stone outcrop, go down the descending access road to the carpark, or park gratis within the narrow lot squeezed next to the highway above, and climb down a graded footpath. If you like, you can take Trail 137, which leads to McCauley Hot Springs, a 45-foot gravel pool with 80-85 degree water. The 1.6-mile hike commences between the gazebo (off to the right) and the river, behind a nailed-down bench, following the stream for 150 yards. The trail then veers left continuing for over a mile along some semi-steep switchbacks that girdle the boulder-strewn hillside. As you work through the pine and oak forest, one broaches a level spot on a ridge with a carved-on tree and campfire traces shortly before the last segment, which trends downward. Keep moving for several more minutes and peer downslope, and to the right. Allow close to an hour one way. According to diverse sources, bathing at the springs takes place both with and without attire.

Battleship Rock

There's a smallish but enjoyable nearby waterfall. Jemez Falls are situated along a short walk through piney woods, best attempted very late March through November, depending on snow. To reach Jemez Falls, go north on Hwy. 4. From the junction of Hwy. 4 with Road 126, continue for 5.5 miles. On your right, the weekend traveler will see a turnoff to Forest Road 133 at a sign that says, not surprisingly, Jemez Falls. If the forest road is not open because the fence is closed (as it may be during the cooler months), you will have to hoof it to the picnic area, about 1.4 miles. The tiny sign for the falls pops up to the rear of the picnic tables. The lovely waterfall cascades at the end of a trail from the picnic ground, which takes just a few minutes; if you have to start from Hwy. 4, the whole stretch might take 45 minutes. Or, from the picnic area, try the fairly easy 2-mile hike along a ridge to the McCauley Hot Springs (approaching it this time from the eastern portion of Trail 137). This trail also begins at the sign for the falls.

Fenton Lake State Park (829-3630) is a sparkling reservoir splendidly lined with tall trees. From the village, head nine miles north on Hwy. 4, and then hang a left on Road 126 for nine more miles (the last mile is gravel). San Antonio Campground appears on the way. Fenton Lake is not large, 35 acres out of the 700 acres devoted to public use, but it provides a wonderful camping-picnicking-fishing refuge stocked with rainbow trout and brown trout. (Note: the trout population declined in 2001 and is now rebounding). Swimming is not permitted here, although canoes and inflatable boats are allowed.

At an elevation of 8,000 ft., Fenton Lake ices over in winter. Summer is the more popular time for camping, and 35 campsites (vault toilets only; several picnic tables; fees $4-14) are spread among the pines and firs. Campsites with RV hookups (6 with electrical/water) are in a loop to the southwest of the lake. Day-use areas on both sides present better views, since they encircle the water more closely. Incidentally, Elijah Fenton was a Presbyterian minister who set up a homestead claim in the 1890s, and this rather remote but well-liked facility based on his property was created in 1984. The construction of a dam during the 1950s backed up the Cebolla River to fill the reservoir. The location was considered to be out-of-the-way enough to serve as the backdrop of a 1976 film, *The Man Who Fell to Earth*. In addition, Seven Springs Hatchery raises fish 3.5 miles to the north of the park on unpaved Road 126. Cross the lake and turn left (if one comes from Jemez Springs) to find pay stations, the ranger office, and overnight use areas south of the ranger building.

The Hal Baxter Cross-country Ski Trail is an easy 2-mile hike that begins just beyond Loop D. Go a tad past the water, and look for a sign on the left, next to the road gate; an RV camp area will be on your right side. The trail partly hugs the treeline, not far from the streambed, following the group camping spots southward, across the Rio Cebolla, and then north again either along the creek or on the road. The little blue stars high up on the conifers are there to guide skiers over the thick snow pack during winter. Info on other trails may be obtained from the ranger. Beavers, squirrels, raccoons, deer, elk, and many bird species frequent Fenton Lake.

Should the weekend traveler persevere on Hwy. 4 roughly 22 miles north of Jemez Springs, you'll eventually run into the spectacular Valle Grande Caldera. It formed as the result of devastating explosions, creating one of the world's largest craters of this type when the volcanoes collapsed hundreds of feet. This vast basin surrounded by mountains (and intersecting a ranch recently purchased for a big price tag as public land) is a million years old. It sprawls into a grassy expanse 176 square miles in size and 15 miles across, now a national preserve. Awesome Redondo Peak at 11,254', a belated volcanic puckering at the caldera's western edge, sneaks into a portion of the view. A few other small volcanic domes, which look like turtle-shell bumps, are also visible.

Talus house / Bandelier National Monument

Bandelier National Monument (open 8-6 in summer, and 8: 30-4: 30 rest of year; admission $10; 672-3861) appears along Hwy. 4, some 38 miles from Jemez Springs. Be warned that this place can be packed in summer. Bandelier contributes another page to the story of turbulent volcanism in the area, as ancient eruptions spewed forth layers of ash that consolidated into soft rock. Forested Frijoles Canyon was eventually etched from this material by the relentless, erosive forces of nature. A circular Anasazi farming village of 300 rooms, Tyuonyi occupied the floor of the canyon from the 1100s-1400s AD, which may be reached via a brief trail from the visitor's center (okay for wheelchairs; allow a half hour). New archeological sites are probably being discovered because of the gigantic Cerro Grande fire that singed Los Alamos in 2000. Other pueblo remnants at Bandelier are currently in need of enhanced stabilization. If you resume the trail, a mild ascent exposes a dramatic view of the Tyuonyi ruins. Short ladders climb up to several preliminary cave openings, lived in at the same time as Tyuonyi. These were talus houses, rooms erected from rock debris (now gone), and backed by these usable spaces in the cliff wall. One has the option to go back at this point. A popular hike to Ceremonial Cave requires that you brave four steep ladders to get inside. This particular site takes in both a small kiva (underground ceremonial chamber), as well as habitation area featuring housing foundations towards the back, a home that might have been shared or defended seven centuries ago. To reach Ceremonial Cave, walk another .5 mile along a shady trail; schedule 1 and .5 hours to visit all three areas. Over 70 miles of additional trails (by permit only) give the adventuresome an opportunity to experience the more isolated portions of this prized monument. A snack bar and gift shop are also available, not forgetting that campers will find developed sites behind the visitor's center.

San Ildefonso Pueblo (455-2273) controls 26,000 acres of stately mesas. The village lies about 20 miles east of Bandelier via Highways 4 and 502, immediately across the Rio Grande. In fact, the folks who lived at Bandelier Monument are the likely ancestors of San Ildefonso residents, who were forced to move closer to the river because of a drought beginning in the 1300s. Despite nagging problems, crops are still harvested in outlying fields, although many have found wage jobs in Española, Santa Fe, or Los Alamos. This Tewa-speaking community, for a time the largest of the Tewa groups, is recognized for its Black-on-black pottery made famous by the late María and Julian Martínez around 1919. These ceramics have become the most successful pottery in the upper Rio Grande during the modern era, helping to launch a pueblo arts revival. Family-owned shops showcasing local artists sell vases, paintings, embroidery, and jewelry. They border the plaza, even now the staging area for vital ceremonials. The church dates to the early 1900s, replacing a structure that was destroyed during the seventeenth century. When the Spaniards reconquered New Mexico after an Indian revolt, tenacious San Ildefonso held out until 1694, one of the last four pueblos to submit. Today, roughly 20,000 visitors trek here annually. San Ildefonso maintains a small museum in the tribal administration building north of the plaza, plus a visitor center close to the pueblo entrance (at the "Y") in the road; permits must be obtained for taking photographs. The major feast day (January 23) is open to the public and celebrated with dancing from very early morning until mid-afternoon. Additionally, dances on Christmas Day and New Year's Day mingle reverence with pageantry to commemorate the holiday season. Watch for yet more dances on Easter Sunday steaming up from 11am or so.

Socorro

Population: 8,300
Elevation: 4617 ft.
Distance from Albuquerque: 77 miles
Chamber of Commerce number: 835-0424

The drive to Socorro takes you down the long Rio Grande Rift. There are only a handful of such continental rifts in the entire world. This one formed as unstable, parallel fault-zones (buckling chunks of the earth's crust) yanked apart, forcing the slivered mid-portion downward. The Rio Grande, which begins way up in the San Juan Mountains of Colorado, flowed through this untidy slash, depositing alluvium and creating a valley. When one flies over southern New Mexico, it is often this life-giving valley that beckons the eye, a startling strand of green interrupting a brown ocean. Even now, commercial pilots use the river as a navigational guide, as did Spanish explorers and Amerindians hundreds of years ago. Today, the area between Albuquerque and Socorro is the most seismically active region of the state, periodically sustaining minor earthquakes. Socorro residents are shaken up by these mini-tremors from time to time. As in much of New Mexico, volcanic activity also contributed to the drama of the landscape. Sierra Lucero, just to the southwest of Belen, was a small volcano. Snow-capped Ladron Peak, an upfaulted block of Precambrian rock and probably the hideout of bad men (*ladron* means thief in Spanish), dominates the skyline to the west of Bernardo.

This portion of the Rio Grande valley was one of the first regions in the United States subjected to European development. Spaniards who had come by way of Mexico sweated to create farms and ranches along the middle river throughout most of the 1600s. Meanwhile Franciscan missionaries endeavored to Christianize local native communities, which were shriveling because of European diseases. Our first stop is La Joya (literally, the jewel). To reach La Joya, get off I-25 at Bernardo. Didio's, a convenience store, has been operating at this lonely spot since 1915. Head east on Hwy. 60 for 3 miles, and then south on NM 304 for 6 miles. The road winds back to the waterway and the tiny village of La Joya. The original Spanish settlement in the vicinity was called Sevilleta (a corruption of Seville), and its San Luis Obispo Mission was established during the seventeenth century to convert the Piro Indians. Sevilleta later referred to a land grant. Currently a wildlife refuge of this name (closed to the public) surrounds La Joya. Look for the sign to the church where NM 304 abruptly ends. Nuestra Señora de Los Dolores, constructed around 1825, stands near the northwest corner of this isolated location, which melts into the thicket along the river. Colonial towns in New Mexico typically huddled near streams to facilitate irrigation. In addition, twelve miles north of Socorro (exit 163), the San Acacia Gallery, once a schoolhouse some ninety years ago, exhibits area artists.

General

Socorro is a good place to learn a little about the history and geology of the state, since it has ties to the colonial, mining boom, and atomic eras. The town is becoming somewhat more attractive, having landscaped the median on the main drag. Socorro preens itself these days with a variety of festivals, including a Fat Tire Rally for mountain bikers in mid-September (835-0424). Many visit Socorro during the cold months in order to see the birds at Bosque del Apache. Snowfall is usually lighter in the mid-portion of the state relative to northern New Mexico. Remember that picnic sites in the adjacent ranges, which receive greater precipitation, will be more accessible by spring. As one moves south along the Rio Grande, the elevation drops from Albuquerque to El Paso by roughly 1500 ft., and summer temperatures will be accordingly hotter in places with lower altitudes. Socorro also represents a warm spot of another type, associated with an important UFO event in 1964, when a shiny oval object landed close to Hwy. 85. Imprints and burns were left behind for physicists to ponder after the craft flew away. The entrance into town lies on old Hwy. 85, the main street known as California Ave., and lodgings proliferate along this stretch not far from turn-of-the-century buildings. A hand painted advertisement for Owl Cigars bedecks a brick structure, the old Knights of Pythias Hall, to your left on Manzanares St.

Socorro started out as a mission village back in 1620s when the Nuestra Señora del Socorro Church was constructed. The name Socorro was inspired when leading settler Don Juan de Oñate passed through the area after trekking the Jornada del Muerto. The notorious "Journey of Death" was a risky shortcut leaving the river's curve and going straight across the desert to the south. Oñate ran ominously low on supplies and water. The Piro Indians vouchsafed him some much-needed corn; hence the spot was so commemorated (*socorro* means help). Even as the mission was being set up, famed chronicler Fray Alonso de Benavides mentioned cheerfully that silver could be removed from the nearby hills. He realized this might slow down conversions, and recommended management by those of only moderate greed, who would pay the natives for their labor. By 1640, Socorro contained 400 souls, but the region was vacated during the Pueblo Revolt of 1680 and not reoccupied until about 1800, encouraged by the Socorro Grant of 1817. Apache ambushes were a constant threat, resulting in 48 deaths during 1836. Silver strikes were made in the Magdalena Mountains commencing a few years after the Civil War and peaking a couple of decades later. Socorro turned into a wild, booming mining town. After the Santa Fe Railroad arrived in 1880, smelters produced hundreds of bars of silver per day. The New Mexico School of Mines was founded in 1889 (or, the NM Institute of Mining and Technology since the 1950s). The Panic of 1893 sent prices plummeting, however, and ranching plus alfalfa production took over. But by now Socorro was one of the state's largest communities, with lots of Victoriana, and it had hatched one of the state's largest legends, namely Elfego Baca, a gunslinger and bouncer turned sheriff and judge. Baca was immortalized in a Disney film of the 1950s, whereas the New Mexico legislature is about to subsidize a Baca statue. Droughts plagued Socorro into the Depression years. Incoming scientists bolstered growth when the White Sands Missile Range, and later the Very Large Array Radio Telescope, were established. New Mexico Tech, the major employer here, continues to train some 1500 students in the sciences.

Practicalities

A hallmark Socorro restaurant is the Val Verde Steakhouse (moderate; 203 East Manzanares; go east on Manzanares from the main street; 835-3380), located in a old hotel. The stylish structure was built in 1919 for railroad passengers (open 11 am-2 pm and 5-9:30 pm weekdays; dinner on Saturdays; 12-9 pm on Sundays; bar service). Other eateries include El Sombrero at the northeast edge of town off the frontage road (210 Mesquite) and Don Juan's Cocina (118 East Manzanares; closed weekends). Martha's Black Dog, just off the plaza (110 W. Manzanares), serves healthy breakfasts, steamy latte concoctions, and homemade soups. The Socorro Springs Public House (115 Abeyta; open 11 am-11 pm Mon.-Sat.; 12-10 pm on Sun.; recommended) bubbles along one block north of the plaza in a nifty historical building, for a time the home of the legendary Elfego Baca. This new entry whips up wood-oven pizza, calzones, and salads, and these folks also make their own beer. Fast food chains abound on the main drag, such as Arby's, Denny's, McDonalds, etc., as well as roadhouse cafes. If you try the scenic byway north of town, the home-cookery of the Coyote Moon Café at Lemitar might come in handy.

Motels are sprinkled along California Ave., the main north-south thoroughfare. The Super 8 ($50 range; 1121 Frontage Road; 835-4626) and the Holiday Inn Express ($80-100 range; 1100 N. California; 838-3900; pool) hang at the north end of town. The Vagabond Motel ($30 range; 1009 N. California; 835-0276; takes pets) represents a budget choice. Econo Lodge ($50 range; 713 California; 835-1500; pool) and Days Inn (about $40 but subject to change; 507 N. California; 835-0230; donuts in a.m.) are in the middle near the San Miguel Mission. With a small pool towards the back, the San Miguel Inn (835-0211; about $50) sits on the east side of California Ave. Meanwhile Motel 6 ($40 range; 807 S. Hwy. 85; 835-4300; takes pets; seasonal pool) crops up at the south end of town. Eaton House Bed and Breakfast, over 100 years old, has private bathrooms (403 Eaton Ave.; 835-1067). Casa Blanca B and B, a revamped piece of the 1880s, keeps guestrooms a couple of blocks from the Owl Restaurant in the village of San Antonio (may be closed in summer; 13 Montoya St.; 835-3027). The Socorro RV Park operates on the Frontage Road (835-2234), whereas there's a Kiva RV Park close to Sevilleta (1-877-374-KIVA). The Bosque Birdwatchers RV Park is also available near the Bosque del Apache on NM 1.

Things to do

The best-known landmark in Socorro is the San Miguel Mission (n. of the plaza at 403 El Camino Real; go west on San Miguel one block from California Ave.). It nested on the royal road from Mexico to Santa Fe at the erstwhile pueblo of Pilabo. The original building (ca.1615-20s) claimed 7-foot thick walls and was called Nuestra Señora del Socorro de Pilabo. Though partially destroyed during the Pueblo Rebellion, the

San Miguel Mission

roofless walls were still standing in 1692, and a recognizable ruin of some sort existed throughout most of the 1700s. The old mission is probably incorporated in the current nave to an extent. Rumors of silver communion rails and other treasures, hastily buried in the scary advent of the revolt, have spurred the romantic and the avaricious to hack up this area over the years. Today's church was constructed between 1800-1820 and renovated in the 1970s. It holds a staircase from the 1850s, carved wood choir loft, adobe bell towers, and several sub-floors, beneath which crypts have been detected. Manuel Armijo, the infamous governor who fled the American takeover of New Mexico during the 1840s, is thought to be interred in front of the facade. The mission's name may have been changed to San Miguel because of an Apache attack, common in the 1800s, when a parishioner beheld a miraculous vision of the warrior Archangel Michael above the doorway. The city celebrates the San Miguel Fiesta in September.

Other noteworthy buildings in the San Miguel Historic District are clustered near shaded Kittrel Plaza, an activity hub named for a local dentist of the 1880s (go west on Manzanares from the main street, or proceed south from the mission through an interesting area for three blocks). Once there were a couple of plazas; this one was fed by a spring from the mountains. The Hilton Block of the hotel family greets you on the northeast side of the square, dating from the 1880s and remodeled in the California Mission style during the 1930s. The Chamber of Commerce reigns here now. To the north, the García House (at 108 Bernard and presently an abstract company) is a stately courtyard adobe from Mexican era. The walls, some twenty inches thick, had leaked away over the years beneath the intact plaster. Thankfully, this problem was discovered and remedied by the current owners before the structure caved in. Conrad Hilton's aunt lived in this house for a time.

The García Opera House (1886) faces Abeyta one block to the north of the plaza. Fischer St. (north side plaza) sets forth a row of older cottages as you gaze to the west for a block or two; the Torres House (225 Fischer) is a classic bungalow from 1913, built of adobe but with mail-order trim. The pueblo-style Socorro County Courthouse lies a dab to the south of the plaza. The Capitol Bar (ca. 1890s) at the southeast plaza corner was redone in the 1990s to accommodate the folks who could not forsake "going down to the Capitol" for a nip. Look for bands here on weekends. By car you can easily reach the Abeyta House (take Park on the plaza's west side and go three blocks south), a remnant of the Victorian boom years. It's now called Casa de Flecha. The Eaton House B and B rests a block west on Eaton (backtrack .5 block and head west on McCutcheon). This place, a Victorian adobe, displays starwashers on the outside, actually reinforcing rods installed after the earthquake of 1904. Socorro's first brewery and a product of the mining era, the Hammel Museum stands on the east side of California (600 Sixth St., several blocks north of the haunted Valverde Hotel). It opens the first Saturday of the month. Contact the Chamber for Commerce (835-0424) for a small map of these areas free of charge.

The Mineral Museum (835-5420; free admission) at NM Tech is open weekdays from 8-5 and Saturdays from 10-2. It contains an outstanding rock collection—some 12,000 specimens—from all over the world, but focusing on New Mexico. These bones of the earth will help anyone to appreciate the color and beauty of the state's extraordinary geology. From the 900 block of the main street, turn west at the Kentucky Fried Chicken onto Bullock.

The Hammel Museum / ice-house & first brewery in Socorro

Proceed through the four-way stop and simply flow with the road's curve onto the shaded campus, watching for the sign on the left.

Several adventures in the vicinity

To the north, Socorro and the BLM maintain the Quebradas Scenic Byway. This trek into some arid, pinkish-red canyons flecked with creosote bush is best enjoyed during the temperate seasons rather than in really hot weather. Rock collectors hike the area, and a few ranchers run cows over the rugged, thirsty hills. Take the Escondida interstate exit and follow the pavement as it gradually winds to the left (north). Go right (east) at Escondida Lake Road, passing a pretty pond and the inviting grove of trees at the Rio Grande, to Pueblitos. The asphalt will phase out soon. Keep right and drive nearly a mile to a fork that has the scenic byway sign. Turn left onto Quebradas Road, and continue 11.2 miles to another fork (stay left). If you want to stretch your limbs, you'll find a parking opportunity in .7 mile on another roadbed branching off of the main route. The attractive Arroyo de las Cañas unfolds before you, roughly 15 miles or so from the point of origin at the interstate (the BLM in Socorro at 835-0412 sometimes has additional info). Passenger cars can probably handle the washboard to this point (employ your own judgment), but one or two of the upcoming washes will be too wide and bumpy for anything but a high clearance vehicle. The scenic byway signs will guide the weekend traveler as they stick up here and there, although they eventually start to face cars approaching from the opposite direction. As one plows forward, a couple of awesome mountain vistas thunder up to the right. The Quebradas Road ultimately splices into A- 129 (veering right), thus returning to Hwy. 380. Hang another right (west) at 380 to reach San Antonio after 10 miles. The whole Quebradas ride adds up to about 32 miles, of which 29 are unpaved.

To the south, the most well known spot is undoubtedly the Bosque del Apache National Wildlife Refuge (835-1828), 94 miles from Albuquerque and 8 miles south of San Antonio. Get off I-25 at San Antonio (exit 139) and head south on NM 1, or, motor south on California Ave. to pick up NM 1 from town. The Visitor's Center is open 7:30 am-4 pm weekdays and 8 am-4:30 pm weekends, but the 15-mile auto loop (cost $3) is accessible from one hour before sunrise to one hour after sunset. This distinction is important, since the birds that gather here from November through February are most visible either prior to their dawn take-off, when they leave to reconnoiter for food, or during their return at dusk, when wave after wave circle and descend into a series of ponds. The north pond often splashes with the greatest activity. The relative chilliness of a particular autumn seems to affect how swiftly the birds actually show up at this winter retreat. An early arrival may signal a serious winter ahead. From one fall to the next, the turnout can vary from pleasing to nothing short of astonishing. The famous migrating fowl that come from the Canadian Arctic, the northern Rockies, and the Midwest include tens of thousands of snow geese, sandhill cranes, and even a few rare, 6-foot-tall whooping cranes.

The sandhill cranes, about four feet in height and colored gray with a red spot at the eye, may be seen soaring over Albuquerque in "V" formation the last few days of October or early November (note: they sometimes make a pit stop in the open fields of Corrales next to the river). The sandhills are among the oldest living bird species on the planet. They mate for life and survive some 20 years in the wild. Several raptors such as bald eagles (topping out at 50 eagles by January) also frequent the area, along with the resident population, or 300 bird species in all. Short trails trickle off from the car circuit. The 57,000-acre refuge was begun in 1939, a byproduct of the Depression. The Festival of the Cranes, initiated by avid conservator Phil Norton during the 1980s, pulls in many people from mid to late November, and the city of Socorro coordinates art shows, lectures, and historic open-house tours at this time (check the García Opera House on Abeyta, the Macey Center on Bullock at NM Tech, or call 835-2077, 835-0424). The late Roger Tory Peterson, the author of internationally acclaimed birding guides, was a regular. Bring binoculars.

By the way, in 1998, a new trail was created a mile north of the Bosque del Apache Visitor Center. The Youth Conservation Corps worked hard to blaze a track west to Chupadera Peak, a 6,195-foot tall desert mountain. The dirt road to the trail is marked from NM 1 by a teeny sign on the west side, and it runs for about a half-mile, dipping under a railroad trestle to the parking area. This hike is 4.75-miles long one way, bordered by stones and a dry streambed, and snaking through changing desert grasses and scrub. At the 1.5-mile point, you will encounter a fork with a bench overlook. One branch reaches eastward back to the parking lot (equaling a 2-mile loop and not the three-mile jaunt shown by the plaque). The other marches to the top, over three miles distant, and one must backtrack from here. There isn't much shade, so bring lots of water if you try this in hot weather.

The area is more appealing in the softer light of a fall morning. Mormon tea and various types of cactus accompany you. Junipers grow on the northerly slopes that hold scant precipitation longer than south-facing hillsides. Rabbits and other small mammals in search of moisture gnaw on pads of prickly pear cactus. Watch out for flash floods after a rain when you pass through a tunnel beneath the interstate. The trail follows a series of canyons formed by volcanic flows of molten rock that sizzled and cracked 33 million years ago within the Chupadera Wilderness. From the summit, check out the San Mateo and Magdalena Mountains to the west. The descent captures a grand overview of the Bosque del Apache Refuge. There ought to be a few brochures at the trailhead, but otherwise inquire at the visitor center for more on this hike.

If this exercise isn't enough, another alternative pops up maybe 1 and .5 miles to the south of the visitor center. Keep your eyes peeled for the Canyon Trailhead on the west side of NM 1.

The weekend traveler should be aware of other nearby sights. South of Socorro, myriad visitors fuel up with a requisite green chile hamburger at the Owl Restaurant (open since 1945 to handle defense workers; closed Sundays) in San Antonio. This place really hustles the Friday after Thanksgiving with Bosque visitors. Manny's Burgers has been here for quite a while also, and, not to be outdone, Manny has put up a gigantic sign. There's an antique store a block south on NM 1; you'll find a gallery or two as well. One gas station sells Carrizozo cider. The village, named for St. Anthony of Padua, was the home of Conrad Hilton, who lived at his parent's boarding house at Sixth and Main. San Antonio, once called Senecu, was originally a stopping point for the remarkable mule caravans that serviced New Mexico's seventeenth century missions.

Other historical remains hint at later efforts to work the habitable parts of this region. Heading east of San Antonio for 1.5 miles and crossing the river, you hit a paved road to the south. Here one can reflect on the adobe ruins of San Pedro, a semi-ghost town and half-hidden church from the 1800s-early 1900s. The cemetery slips into sight immediately after the turnoff. A few folks reside within this short route, along with a number of quail that flutter about the crumbling roofless walls. San Pedro supports a little country store. Carthage is situated 8.5 miles east of the Owl Café, south of 380 behind a mostly-locked metal gate (close the gate if you get in). A state sign indicates this forlorn dot on the highway. San Pedro was an oasis, an agricultural hamlet that made wine and champagne. Carthage, by contrast, was a thriving mining community that produced coal from the 1880s-1940s. It now displays a mosaic of tinted glass shards and a cemetery. A few miles beyond Carthage, the Trinity Site sits to the south of US 380 on Range Road 7, a.k.a. NM 525. This place is not far, ironically, from the deadly stretch of desert that almost unstrung the Oñate colonists of 1598. The location of the world's first nuclear explosion, which occurred in July of 1945, becomes accessible the first Saturdays in April and October from the Stallion Gate,

The remains of Fort Craig

itself the inspiration of novelists. The Trinity Site Open House permits self-guided tours from 8-2 pm (call 678-1143 for info). A stone monument marks the test spot, once accompanied by a statue of La Conquistadora (Our Lady of the Rosary, also called Our Lady of Conquest), put there by spiritually concerned locals.

One can then drive south on NM 1 from San Antonio for 23 miles (you can likewise get onto NM 1 from the San Marcial interstate exit). A washboard road pointed east for 4.5 miles takes you to the visible, if fallen, adobe and plastered rock walls of Fort Craig (1854-1885). The river gleams just beyond. Fort Craig was one of the best-garrisoned posts in the state, and the recruits were supposed to protect travelers or herders crossing the desert. Yet in 1863, confederate troops defeated soldiers from Fort Craig at Valverde Crossing (the village of Valverde, abandoned but on private property, is seven miles back up NM 1), during New Mexico's brush with the Civil War. The men assigned here also tried desperately to subdue marauding Navajos and Apaches, who enthusiastically routed the American military. At other times, monotony resulted in drunkenness and the unauthorized firing of pistols at almost anything. The fort witnessed a well-supplied if hard life, but now seems eerily still. The Bureau of Land Management maintains a good interpretive trail but no visitor facilities.

To the west of Socorro are some popular recreational areas. Box Canyon, at the foot of the Magdalena Mountains, has become a prime destination for rock climbers. Box Canyon unrolls eight miles west of town along US 60. There's a tiny sign on the highway's south side 100 yards before a bridge, and a parking lot of sorts becomes visible to the left after 2/10 mile. Waterfall Wall, a relatively easy climb, is directly to the right of the carpark. Non-climbers will savor watching others defy gravity. You can hike into this craggy rhyolite canyon or drive further south for more rock ascension opportunities; take heed that the setting is mostly treeless and will be more agreeable in mild weather.

Or, proceed west on Hwy. 60, some 16 miles from Socorro, to marker 124. Turn left on paved Forest Road 235 to the large Water Canyon Campground (watch for the sign). Batches of Apache Plume, once used to fix everything from limp hair to sore muscles, nibble the roadway. There are primitive restrooms, but no water, at this camping site, which appears after five miles, as you enter the Magdalena Mountains. A brief walk leads to picnic tables among the trees from the rear parking area. This smallish steep range contains a granite core. Magdalena Peak (8,152 ft.), a bare volcanic cone on the west side overlooking the town of Magdalena, purportedly reveals the profile of a woman's face (that is, Mary Magdalene, according to Spanish legend). The highest point, South Baldy, rises to 10,783 ft. For a cheap thrill, drive up the unpaved road for 10 miles from the campground almost to the top (the track gets rougher as you progress). The gates belong to Langmuir Laboratory, a private NM Tech facility that studies lightning and thunderheads. New Mexico enjoys the quizzical distinction of being second in the nation for lightning strikes. Hikes such as North Baldy Trail are close by, threading into the forest (the Magdalena Ranger Station of the Cibola National Forest sells maps for $6; 854-2281).

Magdalena (elevation 6548 ft.) lies 27 miles west of Socorro, fine for a weekend visit when in the mood to take on a couple of remote locales at a leisurely pace. Frankly, this small community, though quiet, looks less like a ghost town than it did a few years ago and encompasses a population of about 1,000. NM Tech and Cambridge University plan to build an observatory here. An info center has opened on the north side of the highway. Magdalena got started with a railroad spur constructed in 1884 to service miners, cattlemen, and sheep ranchers. Wool used to be an important commodity until displaced by synthetics. Although part of the town was destroyed by fire during the first half of the 1900s, the old train station is now the town hall. It's located behind Evett's Café and Fountain, a popular stop on the main drag (that is, US 60, which becomes First St. in town), open daily 11-8 for burgers, burritos, and shakes. Evett's operates in a redbrick edifice dating to 1906. Evett's still honors the grand tradition of the banana split. The stools at the counter have been twirling since the 1930s.

The vintage hotel, south on Spruce, has undergone an award-winning renovation and is currently a deli, open every day. The mercantile building remains impressive, and the sometimes-open Boxcar Museum (next to the train depot behind Evett's) inventories historical artifacts. A small theatrical troop (London Frontier Theatre; 854-2519) provides seasonal entertainment at the WPA gym, some three blocks south of the highway between Fourth and Fifth (which parallel US 60) at Main Ave. Next to the gym, the Roosevelt Art Center, an elementary school experiencing a facelift, hosts craft fairs and shows. The Magdalena Café at the west end of town makes a basic breakfast or lunch. The Ponderosa Restaurant on the south side of the highway cooks up standards. There are a handful of galleries, even as rock shops showcase blue smithsonite from adjacent mines. The Western Motel (404 First St.; 854-2417; $40 range) usually bakes a.m. rolls and scones, while most rooms come with a frig, microwave, and cable. An RV park is to the back. Across the street, a gallery plus cable TV enhance the High Country Lodge (854-2062; about $45; microwaves; takes pets for $4). Rancho Magdalena, a B and B with a weaving studio, crops up three miles further down Hwy. 60 (mile 109). Magdalena puts on an Arts Fest in early June and the third weekend in November (loosely timed with the Crane Festival) exhibiting painters, weavers, and highly specialized craft artisans from all over the Southwest. The Old Timer's Reunion occurs the weekend after July 4.

One or two options exist north and south of Magdalena. To the north, Road 160 runs for 32 miles into the Alamo Band Navajo Reservation. Crafts are sold during Alamo Indian Days in October (854-2686). Or, visit the ghost town of Riley, a coal mining nook from the 1890s. Sheep ranching, a little farming, and manganese production also helped to sustain Riley during its fleeting heyday. Fossils can be scouted in the hill behind the stone school-

house, which haunts Riley's rear flank; look for the old church and grave-
yard. The apple trees burst into white blossoms during the spring. Locals
celebrate a mass for the feast of Santa Rita here on May 22, though the actual
Santa Rita Fiesta takes place Memorial Day weekend. To get to Riley, hang a
right (north) on the street headed north from the middle of town, behind
Evett's. Bear right onto a nicely graded dirt road immediately before the
rodeo fairgrounds (F.R. 354; the mileage on the sign is wrong) and continue
for 20 miles. Passenger cars should be all right if you move slowly over the
washes. Bear to the right once again upon approaching the Rio Salado, where
you must stop, as there aren't any real parking turnouts. One can hoof it
.75 mile across some flats and over the wire fence to reach the empty streambed. Be careful along its banks, and think twice if the river is flowing due
to a recent storm. Or, truck left (west) at the fork, past a ranch and the river,
up an incline, taking a right at the rustic sign, then another right at a post
marked as a bus stop(!), in effect curling around from the north (and adding
5 miles). The first alternative exercises your feet. Yet the other is a little
harder on your car since the track degrades beyond the creek (ok for sedans
only under dry conditions). Don't get within shouting distance of the church
because the building seems to be occupied at present. The scene remains
photogenic, nestled among arid hills and isolated ranges that fall into the
horizon.

On the other hand, south of Magdalena, the once-competing mining
hamlet of Kelly rusts away in the sun. Turn south at the ranger station, a
good source of trail info incidentally, onto Kelly St. (also marked as Poplar),
from the main thoroughfare. In 2 miles, veer left at the smelter foundation.
You will soon spy the small Catholic church. The cholla cacti along this
route assume a spectral cast when they collect snow during the winter. The
wood and metal skeletons of the Kelly Mine emerge some distance off the
roadside further on (3.5 miles from town). Kelly was begun in the 1870s. It
was named for Andy Kelly, who ran a nearby sawmill. Kelly was tipped off to
the area's potential by J.S. Hutchason, a veteran prospector. Kelly staked a
claim that produced low-grade ore for several years. In the meantime
Hutchason had lots of perseverance, but not the best luck. He gradually sold
off his struggling mines to other adventurers who struck real pay dirt, and a
silver rush soon followed. New saloons and dancehalls bustled to accommo-

date the flush of traffic. The hotel quickly prospered by renting beds in shifts. Crime escalated in proportion to economic activity, and suspects were frequently hanged from the closest convenient tree. Tons of silver ore were freighted from Socorro to Kansas City. Smelters were built, roulette wheels spun, and the champagne overflowed, while special trains imported liquor from California. It's now difficult to imagine Kelly as either a fleshpot or the scene of numerous shootouts. When the silver riches sputtered and died, zinc and lead kept Kelly afloat until the 1930s and by then, these mountains had poured out over thirty million dollars worth of minerals.

Continuing west on Hwy. 60, one traverses the wavering grasses of the voluminous San Agustín Plains, a Pleistocene lakebed known for meteor showers, ranches, and antelope. A couple of camping venues should appear (on the Montona Ranch), one of them shortly before the next turnoff. Twenty miles from Magdalena, the Very Large Array Radio Telescope comes into view, the world's most powerful facility of this type, and featured in the 1997 film *Contact* as well as the 1996 film *Independence Day*. Obviously moviemakers love this place. Motorists must cruise for four extra miles to hit the visitor center with its astronomical photos, open daily 8:30 am-dusk. This may be the only facility in America decorated by tiles of Saturn in the restroom. An odd spectacle, there are 27 parabolic dishes, each 82-ft. across and weighing a hundred tons. Arranged in the shape of a "Y" over eleven miles, they pick up very faint radio waves from deep space emitted millions of years ago. The interpretation of these signals yields a tempting glimpse into the galaxy when it was young, some 10-15 billion years in the past. The VLA is second only to the Hubble Telescope in attracting attention to recent U.S. "astro-technological" efforts. Scientists descend on the VLA from all over the globe, so scoop up a brochure to amble around on the self-guided tour.

Pecos

Population: 1,500
Elevation: 6950 ft.
Distance from Albuquerque: 77 miles
Pecos Clerk's Office: 757-6591
Pecos Historical Park: 757-6032

You can reach Pecos by blasting up I-25. The drive through Galisteo on Hwy. 41, however, might be more peaceful, if several miles longer. The week-end traveler will blip through Stanley, once the location of a couple of hotels, and currently the home of former Governor Bruce King. Beyond Stanley, the heavily-mined Ortiz Mountains, Lone Mountain, and Davis Mountain will be to your left, with White Bluffs to the right.

This undulating tide of short grasses and cholla is part of the Galisteo Basin. The basin is a low area where ancient sediments accumulated, overlain by some volcanic material. Cattle graze this green and pale gold transition into the Great Plains, which is drained by a network of arroyos plus Galisteo Creek. The spot was settled first by groups of prehistoric Indians, and Galisteo Pueblo (ca.1300-1700 AD) eventually mushroomed into 26 housing blocks containing well over 1600 rooms. Then Spaniards tried their luck incrementally during the seventeenth century. Cultural clashes, common in this era, quickly ignited. The mayor of the Galisteo region strained to resolve problems between the clergy and the Amerindians, when one of the friars was accused of abusing his native charges. Galisteo was formally founded in 1706 at the same time as Albuquerque, and by the 1740s, the place supported 50 families, a mission, and several ranches. The standing church dates to 1882. Arthur Godfrey lived here for a while. Rambling adobe homes and artist studios open during mid-October for a tour (call 466-3827.)

The radiant Sangre de Cristo Mountains arise in front of you as an enticement to keep headed north. A belt of Ponderosa pine suddenly emerges.

Glorieta Mesa is just to your right, and after a short section on the interstate, you should get off at Glorieta (exit 299). A few miles east, the village of Pecos ravels around the intersection of the east-west Pecos Road (a.k.a. Hwy. 50) and Route 63. The latter goes north into the canyon or south to the Pecos Monument. Several establishments can be found on either side of the Pecos Road, which connects Glorieta with Pecos proper. The Pecos Road cuts through Glorieta Battlefield, the site of a famed Civil War confrontation in 1862. Texas Confederates mounted an assault actually designed to capture Santa Fe, but they were defeated near Glorieta Pass. The National Park Service has recently purchased the Arrowhead Lodge, once a boy's school, in the vicinity. The setting will soon be turned into a visitor center displaying newly discovered Civil War artifacts. The Santa Fe Southern (989-8600), by the way, runs scenic day trains from Santa Fe to Lamy during most of the week, should you have extra time.

General

Pecos has been a community of one type or another for hundreds of years. By the 1400s, the people of Pecos village had become a successful regional power by virtue of serving as middlemen between the Pueblo Indian farmers of the Rio Grande and the hunting tribes of the plains. Pecos Pueblo, which subsisted on corn, beans, and squash, was some five stories high with a population of two thousand or more. Coronado tarried here in 1540, while Spanish missionaries arrived 81 years later to construct an outstanding church. Pecos became an important Spanish frontier post. Regular trade fairs persisted for many years, the nomads exchanging leather goods or hides for foodstuffs, blankets, pottery, and much later on, even coveted metal items brought in by the settlers. The Pecos Indians were also trained by the Hispanos to be fine carpenters. Eventually, European diseases wreaked their drastic toll on native peoples as the colonial era progressed. An Hispanic community was founded by around 1700, but was mostly smothered until the governor struck up a peace treaty with the warring Comanche after a decisive battle. Several land grants ensued during the later 1700s or early 1800s, invariably accompanied by brooding boundary disputes. Though a mission was reestablished after the Pueblo Revolt, the decimated Indian settlement collapsed, and in 1838 the last survivors trudged off to join relatives at Jemez Pueblo. Caravans following the Santa Fe Trail often rested here, the incoming Americans startled by the decaying ruins.

Pecos—known briefly as Levy during the middle 1800s—lost its status as an exchange center, and came to depend on farming, ranching, and mining, when the locale began to mature once more into a real town. The Pecos River Forest Reserve goes back to 1892, possibly the oldest national forest in the Southwest. Nearby Cowles evolved into a fishing resort. During the 1920s, residents were employed by the American Metals Company to mine the mountains. The Pecos Mine at Tererro produced whopping quantities of zinc, gold, silver, and lead, amounting to some $40 million. The "suburb" of Tererro claimed 3,000 citizens at this time and a great baseball team. Only a few concrete foundations remain. Alfred Kidder meanwhile excavated the pueblo remnants (now the Pecos Monument) in one of the more famous archeological recoveries in the West, resulting in a classification system still used to organize New Mexico's prehistory. Rowe, a microdot south of the monument at the interstate, was already in place, commemorating a contractor for the Santa Fe Railroad. Dude ranches budded along the Pecos River, as locals realized the area's recreational potential.

Pecos is today a small community of adobes and trailers spread along the fertile fields of the Pecos River. The Hispano heritage is strong. Many folks work for some branch of the forest service, cut firewood, or raise livestock. Horses munch in the stubble of modest crops. The region, long a holiday hub, is absorbing more and more developmental spillover from pricey Santa Fe, and lodging is becoming more expensive. The San Antonio del Rio Pecos Church, on the east side of 63 as you drive towards Cowles but facing the river, boasts a tall steeple and a Mexican baroque painting of Our Lady of the Angels, a gift from the Spanish king. The image was painted by Juan Correa during the 1700s and housed originally at Pecos Pueblo. The church, built of stone in 1906, conveys some gothic styling. The town's religious feast day is the first Sunday in August.

Summer is the preferred time if you want to enjoy the emerald forests of the Santa Fe Mountains and southern Sangre de Cristos within the Pecos Wilderness, and campsites may be crowded. A couple of fires within the last few years were far enough away to leave facilities alone. Cabins are popular during the warm months, run as mom and pop operations for the most part. Yet early to mid-autumn can be gorgeous, as the trees within the lower elevations closer to Glorieta and the village of Pecos change to their showy fall colors. Rates should be a little lower, while most of the seasonal restaurants are still open. A rodeo takes place in Pecos during September. Eldorado sponsors a Fun Run in September as well. Reopening the Pecos public pool has been a subject of heady local debate, an issue of potential interest to people who want to stay here for several days. Cross-country skiers may wish to brave the Route 63 area during the snow months, when the roads at Cowles make for good trekking (note that facilities at Cowles are closed in winter). The Pecos Monument remains open all year.

Practicalities

There are several eateries in the vicinity, but their hours can vary seasonally, so bring some supplies, particularly if you rent a cabin. Renate's Restaurant (recommended; open 11:30 am-1:30 pm for lunch and 5-8:30 pm for dinner; closed Tues.), on the south side of the Pecos Road near the interstate exit at Glorieta, whips up, of all things, German dishes and pastries in a simple setting. Kristina's (Pecos Road just west of NM 63 intersection; open 7-8:30 pm) serves sturdy New Mexican fare. The autographed picture of James Woods is a leftover from the filming of John Carpenter's *Vampire*, shot around Galisteo. Slightly north on 63, the Beloved Bakery cranks out pan pizza, rolls, etc. The Pecos Grill (recommended; open Tues.-Sat. from May-November1; moderate to expensive) does a trendy dinner entrée, spanning pastas to fish. The grill can be found on NM 63 immediately south of the main intersection. Casa de Herrera (open 11 am-2 pm and 5-8 pm except Mon; 9-1 on Sunday) is also south on 63 and has a patio. Frankie's Coffee Shop (open 7 am-2 pm and 5:30-8: 30 pm) is south on 63 as well, close to the Pecos Monument, a good hangout for breakfast, sandwiches, and a light dinner except on Sunday evenings. The Pecos Drive-In and Dairy Queen (north side of Pecos Road) will keep you in burgers, tacos, and ice cream. The nearby Glorieta Convention Center runs a snack bar and dining room available to guests; it's easy to buy individual meal tickets upon request. The Inn of Pecos (Pecos Road) no longer provides rooms, but you can purchase gas here and mini-mart stuff, or get a pizza for lunch-dinner. Nash's Lounge imports bands during the weekend.

The accommodations of Pecos are somewhat limited, but there are a growing number of choices. The Los Pinos Guest Ranch (757-6213; $100 range covering all meals), about 20 miles up Route 63 at Cowles, is a log cabin resort nestled against the surrounding forest. It operates only during the summer, and the ranch owners will loan you books on nearby trails. Mark Rents Cabins (988-9517; pets ok in most units; $80-300 range; markrentscabins.com) lies only half as far up the canyon on 63. A variety of nice structures are appointed with everything from paper towels to satellite dishes but require a three-night minimum. Close to Tererro, Pecos Place ($550 per week; 757-6193) maintains a two-bedroom rental house that comes well equipped. Pecos River Cabins ($40-95 range; 757-8760; pecosrivercabins.com) has both rustic and modern units. The older cabins are not insulated for cold weather but include kitchenettes and a central bathhouse, whereas newer shelters (open all year) feature kiva fireplaces, kitchenettes, and private bathrooms. Be prepared for a three-night minimum. This hostelry is located next to the river, maybe .25 mile beyond the Route 63 intersection, on the south side of the Pecos Road, which becomes Route 223. The Cake Stand Inn (757-2426), south on 63, offers both guest rooms and meals in a remodeled Territorial Period farmhouse. A stone porch faces the white picket fence. Salamontes Retreat (757-2528) purveys three guest rooms and a Jacuzzi adjacent to the national forest.

In the general area, the Glorieta Conference Center ($50-100 range; 757-6161), a church-oriented convention facility, makes its private rooms with baths available to the public. Rates are cheaper from October through May. The campus, started during the 1940s, consists of a vast complex of attractive buildings, trees, playgrounds, and ponds. A trail threads out from the RV parking area, located towards the back of the expansive grounds (see below). It's a good idea to book reservations during the non-busy times to insure a relative degree of tranquility, or you could collide with an unwieldy horde of teenagers. The out-of-school months, and even the occasional fall weekend, can be jammed. Nearby lodgings also include the Galisteo Inn ($120-200 range; 466-8200), which has changed hands recently. The plank-floor rooms are part of a 200-year-old adobe house, once the bastion of the

Cabin above Terrero

Ortiz y Pino family. The old jail is now a storeroom. Guest suites are named for different kinds of trees, and there's a restaurant on site open several days a week with a light lunch (moderate; 12-2 pm) and ambitious dinner menu (very expensive; 6 pm until closing). Walk-ins are welcome for meal service unless the rooms and cottages are full; summer sees more activity. Take a right on La Vega past the church and look for the driveway. The inviting thicket of greenery at Galisteo will envelop you like an oasis.

The Pecos RV Campground (757-8720) and the La Paz RV Park (757-6012) are south on 63, as you approach Pecos Monument. Townley's RV Park operates within the canyon north on Route 63.

Pecos is a haven for campers, especially on weekends. Chipmunks flit out from the roadside. Route 63 is dotted with a few open areas, both for fishing and camping, run by several different bureaucracies, although vacation homes for Santa Fe residents have proliferated in the verdant depths of the canyon. If you follow NM 63 to the end, the narrow but paved route twists up to several campgrounds. The Cowles Campground will be off to the left, or west, a few hundred yards beyond the Cowles Pond bridge (fee: $6). One can also take a right after crossing the bridge onto paved Forest Road 305. You'll arrive at Panchuela Campground in 1.4 miles. This spot next to a creek is turning into a day-use picnic area, but there are a few tent camping sites and a pit toilet (fee: $2).

Closer to Pecos, Road 122 shoots off to the left (northwest) from 63 as it approaches the Holy Ghost Campground from Tererro. There is a riding stable/hunting guide service in Tererro, if you're interested (757-6193), plus a general store with fishing licenses. Between the store and a mile back up 63, it's possible to catch sight of dumps from the Tererro Mine as far as Willow Creek Campground. Rock hounds have scrounged garnet, tourmaline, pyrite, and lepidolite off the roadside for years. Also, returning to town, the Pecos Road transforms into 223 as one continues east. Route 223 is paved for a couple of miles before morphing into rocky but manageable F.R. 86, which leads to another camping opportunity after roughly 6 or 7 miles. Keep left. This particular site should be open, although the area surrounding Cow Creek Campground has sustained a bit of fire and runoff damage in recent times. Don't try this route after a hard rain. You should be fine if the roadbed is dry and you drive carefully. Various campgrounds typically post a 14-day limit and may charge about $6-7 per night or more. At last inquiry, Cow Creek Campground was actually feeless, but conditions can change.

Things to do

Pecos Monument (757-6032; $4 fee) is open daily from 8-5. This site has been a part of the National Park Service since 1965. Some time later, actress Greer Garson and her husband E. Fogelson donated more land to the facility from their adjacent Forked Lightning Ranch. The visitor center displays an excellent assortment of artifacts and original artwork. The Pecos Valley held the easternmost outposts of New Mexico's sophisticated Indian societies several centuries ago. Pecos Pueblo, one of New Mexico's most vigorous prehistoric villages, was begun during the 900s and consolidated in the 1200s, but enjoyed its greatest influence during the years 1450-1550. Hundreds of whitewashed houses, entered via ladders, were arranged around a plaza with many kivas. After the colonial period was well underway, Fray Andrés Juárez arrived here in 1621 to construct a church to the south of the pueblo. The Spaniards were great proselytizers, and they converted disinclined Native Americans throughout their New World empire, reaching far into the American Southwest. This particular building, decorated with towers and buttresses, required 300,000 adobe bricks, each brick weighing 40 pounds. Some 160-ft. in length, the Pecos Church became perhaps the most

Cicuyé / Pecos kiva and mission complex

imposing of New Mexico's extraordinary mission structures. Though it was destroyed during the Indian revolt of 1680, a second church was built on the same site by the early 1700s, atop the foundations of the first one. Today, roadrunners dash across the roofless walls, which can be seen from a 1.25 mile trail that begins at the visitor center. The path leads through clumps of juniper to reach the ruins of Pecos Pueblo and the mission.

You can also visit the Pecos Wilderness, a 220,000-acre preserve within the vastly larger Santa Fe National Forest (988-6940). This recreation area is the second biggest and most popular wilderness retreat in the state. It contains over a dozen lakes, the headwaters of the Pecos River, and many peaks within the Sangre de Cristos, these towering at 11,000-13,000 ft. above sea level. This range erupted from folding and faulting and runs mostly north-south. The upper elevations are beautiful, and receive some of the heaviest precipitation in New Mexico. A number of trails explore stands of conifer forest, while the extremely lush areas are harder to get to. Several trails may be initiated from Route 63 from roughly May through early October. For example, the well-liked Cave Creek Trail starts behind the Panchuela Campground parking lot (see directions to the campground above). Bypass the tents, cross over Panchuela Creek via the footbridge, and head upstream or northwest, paralleling the water. The junction with Trail 259 (Dockweiler) comes up in .8 mile. Keep left on Trail 288 (a.k.a. Dave Creek Trail); at 1.5 miles you hit the confluence of Panchuela and Cave Creeks. Douglas fir trees reach towards the sun. Mountain Iris and bluebells bloom abundantly in summer. Stay on the path a short distance further to sight two sets of limestone caves. The second set is more visible. It's feasible to approach the cave entrance, but don't enter because of the steep drop-off inside. The view of the caves is interesting, and forms a great turnaround point for the casual weekend traveler. This trail also hooks up with Trail 251 at the 4-mile point to penetrate deeper into the woodland for a trek to Stewart Lake (elevation 10,400 ft.). Try the Pecos Ranger District (757-6121) for more info. The office is situated south on 63 going towards Pecos Monument.

There's a Benedictine Monastery (757-6415) in Pecos, on the left (or west) side of Route 63 as you head towards Cowles, fairly near the Pecos Road. New Mexico has several monasteries (the Christ of the Desert retreat near Abiquiu being the most renowned and the subject of articles in *Life*). The Pecos friars will allow you to amble around or purchase books in a small gift shop; keep your eyes peeled for periodic art shows or lectures here. They also operate a picnicking pond a short distance further up Route 63 to the left. Monastery Lake is six acres in size, and it's often stocked with brown trout. Just follow the brief walkway.

The Lisboa Springs Fish Hatchery (757-6360) sits a little more to the north, on the left. Kids will enjoy the exhibit on the life cycle of you-know-what. This facility, started in 1921, has been closed for a while due to a disease strain that sneaked in from Colorado, but it will reopen soon. Stocking the lakes of New Mexico from these hatcheries contributes a great deal to outdoor recreation, and an excursion among the tanks gives one a chance to contemplate "fish in progress."

You might wish to see the Glorieta Conference Center. Tell them at the booth (if they ask) that you are thinking about staying here. The trail from the very rear parking lot of this spacious setup, which is being widened into an RV campground, winds through a wooded glen to a ghost town. Go past the registration building onto Oak Lane and then Wildflower Lane, and watch for the signs. You will have to park a couple of blocks from the actual trailhead. Get out and walk the brief driveway to the right, passing the growing flock of recreational vehicles. The leisurely, mostly level jaunt to the ghost town, which commences at the gate, is about 3.5-miles long (allow 1.5-2.5 hours one way). Glorieta Baldy is 5.5 miles from the same point of origin, a more challenging hike to a high elevation for those with ample energy and time. Spanish pioneers named this area Glorieta, meaning secluded bower, because of the tongue of forest tucked between rolling slopes. The Santa Fe Trail passed through nascent ranches that swelled into a real settlement when the S.F. Railroad laid track at Glorieta Pass. Sawmills and a silver mining company attracted a few hundred residents. An assembly of Baptists bought property here during the 1930s-1940s, spending millions of dollars on construction for the convention complex over the next several decades. The offices of Rio Grande Press operate on the grounds. A tiny artist's community at Glorieta village has taken over the adobe homes immediately south of the interstate, with a sometimes-open, nonsectarian tavern.

Grants

Population: 8,600
Elevation: 6470 ft.
Distance from Albuquerque: 78 miles
Chamber of Commerce: 287-4802

I-40 climbs upward as it abandons Albuquerque, leaving behind a series of volcanic spouts that rumple the city's western skyline. These sweeping plains are higher than the Rio Grande because of subsidence that occurred as the two sides of a large rift pulled apart, creating a path for the river and uplifting the land at the margins. On the way to Grants, you approach the shallow brown valley of the Rio Puerco, one flank of this rift zone. Prehistoric people wandered the area in restless bands thousands of years ago. Albuquerque ranches that stretched over the west mesa in colonial times occasionally recognized the Rio Puerco as a rough boundary. White gypsum pops out (the Todilito Formation) near Laguna, while the reddish cliffs along the tiny Rio San Jose display multi-hued striations. Eventually black basalt badlands appear, the wrinkled remains of more volcanic activity. Each of these colors contributes to an otherworldly palette as one enters the edge of Indian country.

General

Spanish communities were named for saints or topographic quirks or extended families or flamboyant heroes. Gringo towns were named for capitalists or commodities or Indian tribes or bergs in Europe. Both cultures also made choices designed to flatter royalty. There was an Hispano here first, Jesús Blea, who homesteaded along San José Creek in the 1870s. Then three brothers by the name of Grant founded a camp in this vicinity during the 1880s, as they had contracted to build a chunk of railroad from Isleta Pueblo into California for the Atlantic and Pacific Line. Several towns along I-40 headed west into Arizona basically commemorate this generation of railroad entrepreneurs or employees (Gallup, Winslow, etc.). The local population waxed and waned, and was revived when a dam was built nearby that briefly boosted agricultural production (carrots and other vegetables) by the 1940s.

The interstate exit for Grants leads you into a cluster of chain motor lodges. Stay on this street, and go a little further over the bridge, and you hit Santa Fe Ave., part of old Route 66. Along this road you will find mom and pop motels, a post office, restaurants, the city hall, and trading posts. A large, decaying gypsum factory stands on the south side, a symbol of Grants' flirtation with industry. Pumice was once mined in the area. Then, during the 1950s, yellow rock— uranium—was "discovered" at Haystack Butte several miles to the west by a Navajo sheep rancher. Uranium mining turned out to be risky (for the miners), but it was profitable, owing to national defense strategies and certain ceramic-making technologies. Uranium mines flourished through the mid-1980s, when the demand went down. Plans for nuclear power plants were stalled in many areas because of environmental concerns. This small city, which still caters to ranchers, seems to be courting the tourist trade, having begun to spruce up its main street with some landscaping and sculpture.

Grants is well worth weekend excursions. It is the most convenient place to stay for visiting several regional attractions. Nearby Prewitt has a rodeo on Labor Day weekend (don't miss the hog show). It's possible to combine this event with the Feast of San Esteban at Acoma Pueblo. Acoma's patron saint is honored on September 2 with a wonderful (and pre-Catholic) Harvest Dance. This ceremony, which takes up a good portion of the afternoon, consists of a costumed march through town carried out against the hypnotic beat of drums and little bells. Grants holds a Chili festival in October and a big ski-snowshoe race on President's Day weekend in February. Grants also has two museums, and is planning a "Sky Center" in conjunction with UNM devoted to astronomy and stargazing. Moreover, it's the logical location from which to explore the San Mateo Mountains. The Sandias in Albuquerque are a large fault block, conspicuously slanted at an angle. The San Mateos, by contrast, are actually a vast volcanic plateau. Mt. Taylor, which crowns this ridge, is an enormous cone built up by successive outpourings of smoldering lava some 38 million years ago. Mt. Taylor (11,301 ft.) predominates its surroundings, and is visible from

Albuquerque on a clear day. It is one of four sacred Navajo peaks. Two others are in southern Colorado (Mt. Hesperus and Mt. Blanca), and a fourth rises among the San Francisco Mountains around Flagstaff. Mt. Taylor, named for an American general, was originally dubbed Turquoise Mountain by the Navajo. The small Cañoncito Reservation just west of Albuquerque is Navajo, tentatively settled with Spanish protection about 1818 after a minor Catholic mission failed to convert them. Mt. Taylor, however, sits closer to the main transition into Navajo land.

Practicalities

There are lots of options for spending the night. Best Western (287-7901), Comfort Inn, Travelodge (287-7800), Holiday Inn (285-4676), Super 8 (287-8811), Days Inn (287-8883), Motel 6 (285-4607; outdoor pool), and Econo Lodge (287-7700; outdoor pool) are situated right off the interstate in order to grab the weary road warrior. The national chains (except for Motel 6) charge in the $50-80 range, depending on the season. Holiday Inn, Super 8, and Travelodge have indoor pools. If you go a couple of miles into town, you'll bump into the local motel strip along the main street. The Desert Sun (1121 E. Santa Fe Ave.) and the Franciscan Lodge (1101 E. Santa Fe Ave.) supply very basic accommodation in the budget category (twenty-dollar range), adjacent to a rather noisy railroad track. Across the street on the north side, the Southwest Motel (1000 E. Santa Fe Ave.) and Leisure Lodge (1204 E. Santa Fe Ave.; small outdoor pool) provide decent, no-frills rooms in the thirty-dollar range. The Sands Motel (112 McArthur Ave.), a block north of Santa Fe Ave. (turn north on McArthur), costs a bit more, and is quieter. Most of these places accept small pets, though some want a deposit. The Cimarron Rose Bed and Breakfast (1-800-856-5776; 689 Oso Ridge Rte.) on NM 53 manages two suites containing kitchens and private entrances, next to a pine forest. Additionally, there's a Zuni Mountain Lodge (862-7616) of nine rooms, with guided tours available upon request, near Thoreau, 28 miles to the west. This place is actually hidden closer to the mountains off of NM 612, with access to the western side of Bluewater Lake. El Morro Café (783-4612) on Hwy. 53 advertises cabins and camping. There are several RV parks in Grants, including Cibola Sands (1-888-264-5229) and Lavaland (287-8665).

One also has a reasonable selection of restaurants. China Gate (105 W. Santa Fe Ave.) turns out a budget-priced lunch and dinner buffet. El Cafecito (820 E. Santa Fe Ave.) is a popular spot for New Mexican dishes. El Jardin (319 W. Santa Fe Ave.) serves southwest food with beer and wine, as does the long-standing Monte Carlo, a Route 66 landmark from the 1940s (721 W. Santa Fe. Ave). The Uranium Café (519 W. Santa Fe Ave.) is a cute breakfast and burger stop. Grants Station (200 W. Santa Fe) knocks out American standards and a buffet. At this writing, the recently-opened Mission Café (422 W. Santa Fe Ave.) presents a light breakfast, lunch, and dinner menu, so you can opt for vegetarian, or go the other way, and build your own sandwich. Coffees, teas, and pastries are obtainable in this renovated rescue mission with its nice hardwood floors and gallery (recommended). La Ventana Steakhouse (110 1/2 Geis St.; go north on Geis from Santa Fe Ave. and proceed one-half block) is a well-established choice for slightly fancier or late-evening meals (recommended). The New Mexican plates and the chicken fajita salad with raspberry dressing are inexpensive; steak and seafood dishes can be moderate to expensive (bar service). There are also fast food/national chain restaurants, plus other local cafes, sprinkled around town. You'll cruise by a big Smiths Grocery Store in the shopping center along Hwy. 547 as it coils north towards Mt. Taylor.

Things to do

First things first. The ride to Grants on the interstate can be vexatious because of the trucks, so you might want to get off the highway at Laguna. Laguna Pueblo is relatively new, and it was relocated to this spot during the late 1600s due to population shifts after the Spanish reconquest of 1693. Refugees from several pueblos coalesced here. The Keres-speaking Laguna people, however, have been in the general vicinity for a very long time, originally guided by their protective spirit, Iatiko, according to legend. Modern archeological recoveries tend to support the oral tradition. The town's slight rise shows off St. Joseph's Church (feast day September19), constructed from 1699-1705, and even now easily spied from the disembodied perspective of the interstate. It houses a special altar screen from 1800s painted by a regional *santero* (religious artist).The pueblo enfolds 5000 inhabitants distributed into six villages. If you roam north on 279, you pass an open-pit, defunct uranium mine. This symbol of modern defense technology forms a bizarre contrast to ancient townsites like Acoma, one of the oldest continuously occupied communities in the United States, predating European settlements by hundreds of years. Today, Laguna Industries is in the process of fulfilling a $30 million contract to work on U.S. Army mobile control stations. At the end of 279 stands Seboyeta's village church, Our Lady of Sorrows, built about 1820. Seboyeta touts itself as the oldest Hispanic community in western New Mexico. Actually, one or two hamlets were founded along the Rio Puerco during the 1700s, but they withered and died out. A chunk of adobe wall may be seen by walking around, part of an old fortress created as a defense against the Navajos during the turbulent nineteenth century.

Though Indian gaming is controversial in New Mexico, casinos make handy rest stops for travelers. These places are accessible from interstate exits. Laguna's Dancing Eagle Casino (several miles west of the pueblo on the south side of I-40) runs a snack bar serving pizza. Acoma Pueblo's casino and convenience store (go north at exit 102) have become quite popular with truckers, and this complex seems to be expanding. The casino building has clean bathrooms and an attractive 24-hour restaurant featuring buffets—not a bad deal if you are hungry and fill your plate twice. Incidentally, Acoma has just opened a hotel (552-6123) of 120 rooms with a pottery jar-shaped swimming pool.

You can leave the interstate to follow Road 124 into Grants through several pin dots on the map. Road 124 bounces under and over I-40, encompassing hunks of dust-bitten old Route 66. Cubero (started 1833-1834) feels like a postcard from the 1930s Route 66 period. Route 66, remember, was designated in 1926. It connected Chicago to the west coast through Santa Fe via automobile during the Great Depression, a dramatic trek of 2,448 miles celebrated in American literature. Cubero was once a thriving farm community until the droughts of the 1930s and 1940s. The dust blew so badly in 1936 that residents could barely see the sun for days on end. Wind-driven particles mercilessly devoured the paint from automobiles, while blanketing floors, beds, chairs, tables, fields, and buildings. Vivian Vance (from *I Love Lucy*) lived in Cubero, and though the motels are mostly ghosts, you can still buy gas. San Fidel, based on the old settlement of La Vega and renamed during the modern era to acclaim no less than three saints, drew settlers like the Jaramillo family as far back as the 1860s. The San Fidel store dates to about 1915. Once you are in Grants, there are a couple of different attractions.

The New Mexico Mining Museum (closed Sundays except during peak summer season; admission $3; 100 North Iron Avenue) is easy to locate near the civic center on the north side of the main drag. This handsome installation claims to be the only museum devoted to uranium mining in the entire world. It explores the history of Grants in relation to ranching and controversial mining activity with some good artifacts, offering the weekend traveler a chance to descend in a "cage" to experience the strange, subterranean world of a make-believe mineshaft. In addition, you will run across brochures for a variety of area activities in the lobby.

The Dinosaur Discovery Museum (open daily; $3.50-5.50) is pretty new, and to find it one must drive over the interstate a tad to the south of the chain motor lodges, and then head right (west) to the carpark next to the Lavaland RV lot. This facility contains hands-on displays and robotic dinosaurs plus eerie skeletons that will appeal to youngsters and committed reptile fans of all ages. Fascinating dinosaur remains have been excavated in the western portion of the state from time to time. There's a gift shop on site.

Other interesting alternatives within reach

El Malpais National Monument (240-0300; office closed Thanksgiving, December 25, and January 1) unrolls not far from Grants, and it embraces, in bits and pieces, some 376,000 acres. You have to backtrack to the east of Grants for four miles on 124 or I-40, and then go south on 117 for 9 miles to reach the Bureau of Land Management visitor center (there's a second visitor center 23 miles south of I-40 along NM 53). Many folks in New Mexico are astonishingly ignorant concerning just how much of our landscape was shaped by volcanoes. After all, we live in the Southwest, not on the Pacific Rim. But the Malpais (or literally, bad country in Spanish), a black lake of split-surfaced, ropey stone, is mute testimony to the intensity of vulcanism in the area, which commenced at this precise location three million years ago and ended less than 1,000 years ago. Many features bear Hawaiian names, since the study of volcanoes developed in these islands. Kipukas are undisturbed spots that the lava encircled but did not submerge. Smooth lavas are called pahoehoe, whereas rough lavas are known as a'a. A mile south of the visitor center is a turnoff to the west, and a 1.5-mile side road (with picnic tables and restrooms) leads to the Sandstone Bluff Overlook and its fine vistas of the countryside.

Some 4.8 miles south of this turnoff is a fence on the west side with steps to the Zuni-Acoma Trail, an ancient Anasazi trade route. Peak prehistoric occupation here (roughly 950-1300 AD) was connected to activity at Chaco Canyon and later sites to the north. This hike is 7.5 miles one way over to a corresponding trailhead on Hwy. 53, and is harder to follow once you engage the exposed and uneven lava sections (look carefully for the rock cairns). It can take several hours because of the terrain and tends to be hot in summer. This outing should be attempted only with sturdy shoes, drinking water, and preferably a compass. Various surfaces traverse lava outpourings from different time periods with diverse textures (the Laguna, McCarty, Bandera, and Twin Craters lava flows). Be sure to check the visitor center for maps and info. The weekend traveler with limited time can amble part of the way through Ponderosa pine forest in order to broach the badlands, and then return via the same route.

If one continues down 117, after .5 mile (as measured from the Zuni-Acoma trailhead) the sandstone formation of La Vieja, meaning the old woman, arises to the west. Another 2.2 miles later, one will encounter the state's second largest natural arch called La Ventana (the window), a 165-foot long blending of subtle sandstone shades dating back millions of years. This stop contains a .25 mile paved trail and restrooms. From here, the visitor can progress 4.5 miles to the picnic spots at the south end of the Narrows, a slim corridor where lava flowed near the base of a 500-foot cliff. In 7 miles more, you reach the Lava Falls on the west side. A stroll enables one to take in a little of the McCarty's Crater, the youngest lava flow (about 800-2,000 years old) in the valley. Five miles beyond this point, the Chain of Craters Backcountry Byway branches off to the right of NM 117, running west then north to Hwy. 53 (recommended for high clearance vehicles only).

Acoma Pueblo may be the oldest town in the United States. It took shape roughly between 1150-1250 AD. Only one or two pueblos in Arizona declare a similar legacy. You have to drive east from Grants some 11

Enchanted Mesa near Acoma on NM 23

miles (look for the interstate exit and follow the signs), and then head south about 13 miles to reach the pueblo along Acoma Routes 30 and 38. This site might be a good diversion on the way to or from Albuquerque, and NM 23, a better road, makes an approach from the east side (going this way from Grants adds up to 32 miles). Some 6,000 inhabitants live spread out on the reservation, with only 30 families numbering less than 100 persons in Sky City year-round. The tourist center with its exhibits and shops is open at 8 am most of the year (closing time varies seasonally from 4 to 7 pm), but facilities may be dark on special days (June 24, June 29, July 10-13, July 25, and the second weekend in October; admission $7-8; camera fee $10; 747-0181 or 470-4966).

The weekend traveler can walk or ride a bus to the top via a road supposedly built by a movie crew in 1969. The town is perched almost 400 ft. above the surrounding country on a commanding mesa, picked out for defensive reasons. Steps and holes in the stone were once used to negotiate the climb, while cisterns within the summit collected snow and rainwater. Coronado was awed by the rocky ascent in 1540. The indefatigable soldier-colonist Oñate struggled and fumed to bring Acoma into the Spanish fold during 1598-99. The pueblo became the site of tortuous pitched battles resulting ultimately in many deaths, grisly punishments, and then servitude. Some years later, according to one tale, Father Juan Ramírez was attacked by a hail of arrows from the top of the mesa when he first arrived. At that moment, a small girl toppled off the cliff, landing squarely at the feet of the priest. When Ramírez carried the unscathed child up the escarpment, her amazing survival was perceived as a miracle, kindling the conversion process.

Even now Acoma's flat roofs, and its close-together angles plus haphazard textures, don't look like something you would expect to find in the United States. The exterior surfaces must be refinished regularly due to weather extremes. Some have been modernized with stucco or cement, though utilities as such are scant. Watching incoming weather fronts or the dome of the night sky must be remarkable from here. Note that private homes occasionally display pottery for sale. Acoma's white-bodied ceramics have achieved artistic recognition since the 1950s, and there's a respected pottery gallery in Acomita by the interstate.

The massive San Esteban del Rey Mission in Acoma was constructed from 1629-1640. It contains a famed altar and religious art, and the painting of St. Joseph was a gift from the King of Spain. One report from the 1700s mentions that the priest's residence had room for twenty friars! The Indians performed the exhaustive labor on these landmark colonial buildings, in this case dragging ceiling beams with yucca ropes from the slopes of Mt. Taylor, some two-dozen miles to the north. New Mexico's churches from the early decades of the 1600s, and this one in particular, are a national treasure, predating missions in Texas, Arizona, and California by a century, and in some cases, two centuries, invariably catalogued in textbook syntheses of American architecture. Acoma's church, renovated during the 1700s and again in the 1920s by John Gaw Meem, may have endured in part because, although damaged from time to time, it was never subjected to the devastating floods experienced by pueblos along the Rio Grande. Nor was it destroyed during the Pueblo Revolt. Nevertheless, Acoma has had its problems. The pueblo was engaged in endless boundary disputes with Laguna over the course of the nineteenth century. Victorian chroniclers described the houses of Acoma as draped with ristras of chile peppers. Farming continues to be important. Meanwhile three miles to the northeast stands the huge monolith of Enchanted Mesa (on NM 23).

Bluewater Lake State Park (876-2361) is the largest body of water in this portion of the state. It can be reached from either Prewitt or Thoreau, both west of Grants. To find the lake from the closer Prewitt approach, go 20 miles beyond Grants on I-40, take exit 63, and then proceed south seven miles on 412. You'll run into the park fee booth, where rangers hand out small maps. Bluewater Lake, a 2,350-acre reservoir set among low juniper-covered hills, is somewhat murky for swimming (a few folks do swim from the north end). While not necessarily the most picturesque state park, this place is a favorite among anglers aspiring after rainbow or cutthroat trout, or catfish. Actually, the small catfish are a big deal here. A relaxed resort community has bubbled up at the park entrance. At least one country store (the Yah-ta-hey, of debatable spelling meaning hello in Navajo) offers fishing supplies and a modest restaurant with take-out specials. Another outlet (the Lakeside Market) stocks groceries and Indian jewelry. There are three developed campsites, some primitive camping, and a boat ramp to the south of the park station. Another developed campsite peeps into view off a side road to the west. If you cruise the brief drive all the way to the south end scenic overlook, you'll stumble into the 80-foot dam. Built in the 1920s, this structure bottles up the waters of Bluewater Creek. A steep little trail dips from the south end campground to the creek, and another tiny one heads from the last parking area to the lake. Summer through early fall are usually the busy times. Speedboats for water skiers, as well as fishing boats and even canoes, are permitted.

The Zuni Mountains and Bluewater Park may also be checked out from the west by getting off the interstate at Thoreau (28 miles west of Grants), and driving south on 612 for 11.5 miles to the lake entrance. Beyond here, the pavement ends in a little less than two miles, turning into a pretty good gravel road. Remember that the appealing upper elevations will be available only during the warm months (late spring through very early fall). To reach Ojo Redondo Campground, keep going for another 9 miles on F.R. 178. You'll then see a second sign for the campground, which points you left for the final three miles. This is a primitive camping area without water or fees, but the weekend traveler will discover tables and restrooms beneath the shadow of Mt. Sedgwick, the tallest peak in the 70-mile-long Zuni range, measuring at 9,256 ft.

It's possible to connect with the Zuni system of forest roads from the east, by way of Grants. In fact, Grants and the Department of Agriculture have put together a Zuni Mountain Auto Tour (get the brochure at the Mining Museum). Don't do this in a motor home, and make sure you have some gas. This byway is part of an old but important logging trail used from the very early 1900s until World War II. Some 45 million board feet of lumber were shipped to eastern markets from these woodlands. About 1.5 miles from the museum and just south of the interstate along Hwy. 53, hang a right onto Zuni Canyon Road (a.k.a. F.R. 49). The first 4.4 miles into Zuni Canyon are asphalt, followed by an ok gravel road. At this juncture, Stop #1 should be on your right. The cleared path of a log chute becomes apparent to the left after 4.4 more miles. A sign for Ojo Redondo Campground comes up in two miles (the camping area may be reached from this side in 9 miles). Remnants of a railroad bridge are visible in another two miles (Stop #4). Workers earned a couple of dollars a day felling the logs, loading them onto horse wagons, and then driving them to the railhead, which had spurs way into the high country.

Forest Road 49 abruptly changes designations to F.R. 50 in 3.5 miles. You can head south on the gravel part of F.R. 50 to hit Hwy. 53 in 12 miles, or continue the tour by going west (right) on F.R. 50 at this point. Beware that the road to the west is dirt for the next big section (perhaps 25 miles), and will be way too sloshy for passenger cars after inclement weather, so exercise real caution. A young "plantation" of Ponderosa pines sowed by the Forest Service in 1979 quickly emerges (Stop #6), replacing some lost trees. Fierce cutting depleted many stands. Still, the alligator junipers with their gray, platelet bark are considered to be of championship size in these mountains. You then pass through Cold Springs (Stop #7), and can shortcut to F.R. 548 (to the right), connecting with 178 for the ride out. If you stay on F.R. 50, you will see a small area once devoted to dry land farming (Stop #8), possible because of the 22-inch rainfall. Crops were cultivated to feed the camp workers. Stop #10 (milepost 26.6) discusses the geology of the Zuni Mountains. One can take a right on F.R. 480 (which also links with 178 to loop out), or go a dab further up F.R. 50, for Stops #11-13, and then backtrack to F.R. 480. Once you hook up with 178, the road becomes gravel, but expect a couple of quick jogs near Post Office Flats. F.R. 178 evolves into pavement as you enter the Bluewater recreation area; proceed about 12 miles on 612 to reach the Thoreau exit at the interstate. If you do the whole tour, from Grants to Thoreau, you should clock in at something like 62 miles. Note that the Malpais National Monument sells a Recreation Map. It shows the network of forest roads throughout the eastern portion of the Zunis. In addition, one or two of the Cibola Forest Rangers (287-8833) know this region well.

The Ice Cave and Bandera Volcano (12000 Ice Cave Road; open daily 8 am-one hour before sunset; admission $8) appear 25 miles southwest of Grants along Hwy. 53. This lunar landscape straddles the Continental Divide at an elevation of 8,000 ft.. The Zuni Indians tried to sidetrack Francisco Coronado by taking him here. An exploding volcano around five thousand years ago created a spooky, lava-tube cavern. In fact, the 17-mile lava tube system is considered to be the longest one on this continent. At a temperature of 31 degrees, the cave is covered with a perpetual, blue-green ice formation as the result of water that seeped in and became trapped because of the insulating properties of the surrounding volcanic material. The cave is accessible via a staircase. To get there, rove along the little numbered trail from the log trading post. It sells everything from Indian jewelry to pueblo pottery to mineral specimens to Zuni Mountain cookbooks. The adjacent 500-foot-tall Bandera Volcano looms into view along a great short hike (.5 mile) encircling the circumference of its dark crater, about 1,000 ft. across. Parts of the Bandera Flow are thousands of years old, but other sections form the area's second youngest gush of lava. This property was acquired a while back as part of the Malpais Monument.

El Morro National Monument (open daily 9-7 in summer and 9-5 rest of year except December 25 and Jan1; trails roped off 1 hour prior to closing; admission $4; 783-4226) is 41 miles from the interstate along NM 53. Nine campsites (RV and tent) are sequestered in a loop off to the left before reaching the visitor center, which screens a 12-minute video program. El Morro is an impressive sandstone escarpment 200-ft. tall, with cracks that have weathered into noticeable joints. The mesa top was inhabited from the late 1200s to around 1350-1400 by a couple of pueblos, one encompassing over 1,000 people, nurtured by a runoff pool at the rock base. The northeast corner of A'ts'ina Pueblo was excavated during the 1950s revealing stone foundations, these created from slabs hacked out of the soft sedimentary rock and piled on top of each other. The residents evidently abandoned this magnificent location to move into the Zuni valley, leaving behind numerous petroglyphs (rock carvings). A steep, self-guided two-mile trail (allow 1-2 hours) leads to the ruins at the top of the mesa from the inscription rock area. Another shorter, easier walk is actually paved (.5 mile; ok for wheelchairs) and favors a view of various inscriptions chiseled into the escarpment wall. Spanish colonist Don Juan de Oñate carved his moniker on the stone on April 16, 1605 while on his way to the *mar del sur*, or sea of the south, meaning the Gulf of California. His still visible words *pasó por aquí* (passed by here, written in third person past tense with an accent over the "o," a standard remark) have become famous, serving as the title of films and stories. Governor Manuel de Silva Nieto left his signature in 1629. Don Diego de Vargas, who conquered New Mexico after the Pueblo Revolt, also etched on El Morro in November of 1692. Don't expect these graffiti, scratched out in colonial shorthand, to look exactly like contemporary Spanish. Later, when the United States took over New Mexico, an army lieutenant and engineer, James Simpson, visited El Morro. In 1849 he spent two days copying the names while adding his own to the list. Other westward expeditions followed suit.

There are some other archeological sites near Prewitt. Casamero Ruins consist of the wall footings for a small 22-room pueblo that was once part of an ambitious settlement network centered at Chaco Canyon. A big system of "roads" connected these satellite locales, called outliers. Anasazi is the label applied to the prehistoric peoples of northern New Mexico, forerunners of today's Pueblo groups. The compact rooms of this single structure were occupied from 1000 to 1125 AD. An enclosed circular kiva exists within the northeastern portion of the site, whereas another unexcavated kiva lurks some 200 ft. to the southeast. You have to wonder how some of these little communities managed. Water availability in nearby Casamero Draw may have been much more predictable at that time. During the hot months, bunches of purple asters spring from the tawny earth surrounding the site,

Casamero Ruins / a Chaco "outlier"

which is positioned beneath the bulging, fire-red mesas typical of the plateau country. Drive 19 miles west of Grants to Prewitt on NM 122 (paralleling the interstate), and then north 4 miles on McKinley County Road 19. Continue .2 mile beyond the pavement, and look to the left (west) for an explanatory plaque.

It could be added that Casamero Ruins lie within the eastern peripheral or "checkerboard" area of the Navajo Reservation, a mixed soup of federal and privately held lands. Although the formal boundary of the largest Indian reservation in the United States is several miles to the west, chapter houses (governing subunits within Navajo land, of which there are 109) really begin in the general vicinity of Prewitt. The ancestors of the Navajo filtered into the Four Corners maybe 700 years ago, some time after the Anasazi deserted this specific spot. The Anasazi often clustered into multi-family farming communes, some of these becoming huge defensible villages, while the Navajos tended to spread out thinly. Don't be surprised to see Navajos decked out in turquoise in the restaurants of Grants. By the way, Haystack Butte (7833 ft.) , the origin of the uranium boom during the 1950s, erupts a little to the east Prewitt on the north side of NM 122.

If you're hot, go up to the mountains. Mt. Taylor is part of the San Mateo Range. The U.S. Forest Service manages the Mt. Taylor branch of the Cibola National Forest (office in Grants, 287-8833). Camping is available at the Coal Mine Campsite (no permit; small fee); you can also camp further up in the undeveloped areas (no permit or fee required). The volcanic San Mateo

Mountains, with their blackish outcrops of basalt, are home to black bears and elk. On a recent trip, a fellow hiker warned me, as I approached La Mosca (a secondary peak here), about a bear lounging in the middle of Forest Road 453, right under the summit. This particular hiker quietly backed away and decided to complete this last stretch at a future date, a sensible attitude.

A very popular hike up Mt. Taylor can be reached by trucking north on First St., which becomes Hwy. 547. Proceed for 13 miles; the road switches directions once or twice through town. You will be climbing for a few minutes before reaching the terminus of the pavement. Then head right (east) on Forest Road 193. This route is bumpy in spots for regular passenger cars (go slow). After 5.1 miles, slip into the tiny parking area on the right. The small wooden sign for the Gooseberry Springs Trail (#77) should be on your left. Trail 77 ascends for three miles up the last two thousand feet of Mt. Taylor, following an old roadbed in a couple of places. Watch for returns to the winding trial and stay on it. One leaves the conifer forest for an open meadow after a mile or so. The hike is not especially difficult, but you need some time. The trip up can take about 1.5-2.25 hours one way, though the descent goes faster. Attempt this hike only in summer, and bring a canteen. The panorama from the top is really outstanding, especially to the south and east.

Another way to enjoy these mountains is to return to 547. The pavement terminates immediately north of the F.R. 193 turnoff. Road 547 now morphs into F.R. 239 going north. After 3.2 washboardy miles, you run into Forest Road 453, headed right (east). La Mosca crest tilts up five miles from here. There is a fine picnicking area along this route with excellent views. Passenger cars can make it for about three miles. The last two miles to the La Mosca lookout may be hiked, if you don't have a four-wheel drive vehicle. The high evergreen forest of spruces, firs, and aspens swells thickly enough at this point to appear darkly beautiful and mysterious. Communication towers peak out from La Mosca summit. You can go back to Forest Road 239 and continue north for several more miles winding up in San Mateo village. Primitive camping (no fees, no developed sites) is permitted along here and along 453, but stay away from the drinking tanks for cattle, and clean up carefully. Do not leave out food, which attracts scavenging animals.

Cuba

Population: 1,000
Elevation: 6905 ft.
Distance from Albuquerque: 80 miles
Cuba Visitor Center: 289-3808

The drive to Cuba gets you into the Colorado Plateau, named for the Colorado River. This is a gigantic zone spilling all over the four corners, what Tony Hillerman once called the "land of room enough." Ancient seas covered much of this region hundreds of millions of years ago. Oil and natural gas were discovered hereabouts during the 1940s. One finds colossal horizontal blocks of not-so-old pinkish sedimentary rock, streaked with "fingers" of whitish gypsum, interrupted by reddish to dark outcrops of extremely ancient Precambrian granite. The area is also pocked with the hearts of extinct volcanoes.

General

Cuba means cask or barrel or vat in Spanish. The promotional literature from the local tourist office states that *cuba* can also mean draw or trough. In New Mexico, or in Mexico for that matter, it is not unusual to run across the same place designations over and over. For example, Los Alamos (cottonwoods) and Alamogordo (fat cottonwood) both refer to the tree everyone knows from riparian corridors. It is not entirely clear what the town of Cuba has in common with the dominion of Fidel Castro.

Cuba apparently started off in the second half of the eighteenth century as Nacimiento, a handle derived from the surrounding land grant (ca. 1769) given to some three-dozen settlers attracted by the Rio Puerco. Managing the Rio Puerco watershed continues to be an important regional issue. The name Nacimiento (nativity or source) is still used for the granite-core mountain ridge running along Hwy. 550 (formerly Route 44). The area suffered from Navajo assaults, and today, the checkerboard (or non-federal) portion of the reservation is only a short distance away. Resettled in 1879, Cuba counted on logging, mining, and ranching. Cattle drives once traipsed regularly from Cuba to Bernalillo, an adventure that might drag on for a week to go 65 miles. The western slopes of the mountains produced copper and silver from 1881 (or long before) until about 1960. By 1965, the logging industry also suffered a setback due to various legislative measures. Cuba is currently a little run down, and could use a facelift in order to lure more overnighters. Yet for the Albuquerque non-camper, Cuba seems the obvious place from which to mount a weekend tour of the San Pedro Wilderness or Chaco Canyon. A rodeo is held here in June and a county fair in August, while a fiesta usually occurs the first week in September. Ranchers run cows over high elevation pastures in summer.

Some historical buildings have been torn down. Our Lady of the Immaculate Conception Church, from the early 1900s, was destroyed in 1965. Young's Hotel, which still stands on the main street's east side immediately south of El Bruno's, dates to the late 1930s, and has experienced incarnations as a bus stop and private home. A few other adobe and stone structures need rehabilitation. On the other hand, Richard's Trading Company is a stalwart business in Cuba, having opened in 1946.

Practicalities

Cuba is not without its surprises. The above-mentioned El Bruno Restaurant is recommended (open daily 11 am-9 pm). In the Herrera family for over two decades, this place maintains several nice dining rooms, plus a pleasant patio, bar service, and tiny gift shop. El Bruno is a joy in an otherwise low-key gasoline stop. The menu remains comprehensive, with New Mexican dishes (inexpensive) and specialties of the house (moderate).

Most of Cuba's eateries serve basic fare, and they are situated right along Hwy. 550. The Cuban Café, a fixture on the street's west side, turns out New Mexican plates, American entrees, and pies. The Del Prado Café, with its burritos, etc., is on the east side. Preciliano's, at the town's north edge, whips out hearty standards, enchiladas, and homemade cinnamon rolls. Preciliano's Café operates opposite a super busy convenience store/gas station housing a Taco Bell. Other small businesses sell groceries, ice cream, sandwiches, and pizza. At this writing, Cuba's one coffee bar (the Coffee Stop at 38 Main) has become the Eagle Nest Café, cooking up breakfast, barbecue, and burgers. The Blue Star Café, supposedly in the process of starting a coffee patio, makes decent lunch specials and bakery items.

Motels, strung along the highway, are also basic, though they may provide cable TV. The Cuban Lodge (289-3269) sits at the town's south end. The quieter Del Prado Motel (289-4379) is positioned in the middle of Cuba. The Frontier Motel (289-3474), at the north end, is more appealing, but this option has the disadvantage of irregular lobby hours (opening in the late afternoon on weekends), although the management does accept pets. Rooms for two people at these establishments run in the thirty-dollar range. There is also a Circle A Ranch Hotel (289-3350). Meanwhile, the Regina Inn and Café (289-3178), which advertises handmade gifts, lies several miles to the north on Hwy. 96. A bed and breakfast at Nageezi (the Chaco Inn; 632-3646) has taken over an old trading post near Chaco Canyon. You'll find an RV camp a few miles past Cuba on the west side of the highway.

Things to do

Zia Pueblo, cradled in the open valley floor of the Jemez River, arises on the east side of Hwy. 550. You can easily see this village in a few minutes going to or from Cuba. The sun sign on New Mexico's flag is actually the symbol of Zia Pueblo, the subject of vociferous legal debate, since many organizations and businesses use this image. In fact, a recent poll has designated our state banner as the coolest flag design in the nation! Despite terrible upheavals, sickness, and famine, Zia has persevered for hundreds of years. The explorer Antonio de Espejo was impressed by Zia's endless whitewashed houses in 1583. The people were garbed in flowing cotton blankets tied with sashes, their hair often plaited into braids. The locality was even visited by the colonizer Oñate, when the community encompassed several thousand souls quartered into distinct enclaves. This group speaks Keresan and now numbers close to 700. After the Spaniards brought in stock animals, the people supported themselves by raising goats and sheep. Zia inhabitants are known for their pottery with a white background (look for the Cultural Center). The town's feast day is August 15. Other ritual dances are typically held on December 25 and January 6. Zia's Our Lady of the Ascension Church, plastered white with leaping horse motifs, was constructed in the early 1600s and then rebuilt at the close of the seventeenth century or opening eighteenth century. Come during daylight hours only (no photographs). Zia Lake on pueblo property offers opportunities for anglers (permit required; 867-3304).

The Pueblo Indians in this area manage a few picnic and/or fishing spots (not to mention Santa Ana's casino, golf course, garden center, and Hyatt Resort in Bernalillo), these facilities often indicated from the highway. The Hyatt Tamaya runs an elegant café overlooking Tamaya Hill. Meanwhile Holy Ghost Picnic Area is not quite 43 miles from Bernalillo. You must drive a mile over a gravel road to reach the sheltered tables, good for stretching your legs or making that call on the cell phone. The hazy mists from nearby canyons were once interpreted by a settler as a vision of the Holy Ghost, which encouraged the discovery of a little spring that feeds the ponds here.

There is also a significant natural feature close by. On Hwy. 550, almost 42 miles northwest of Bernalillo and before Holy Ghost, look for the road on the left (the west side), marked San Luis-Cabezon. The first eight miles to San Luis are paved. After about 3 more miles on the main route, you'll spot a small parking turnout, and you can either drive or walk the sidetrack to the left. This roughly eleven-mile stretch (from 550) will take you to the town of Cabezon. Cabezon Peak, a flat-topped basalt volcanic plug some 7785 ft. in elevation, grandly presides over the region (*cabezon* means head in Spanish). The Navajos claim the landmark was once the head of a giant that, having been lopped off by twin warriors at Mt. Taylor, rolled eastward to this location. The giant's knotty dark blood slowly solidified into the lava beds around Grants. The local Hispanos obviously respected this imagery when they named their ranching community, now the ghost village of Cabezon. Spanish pioneers were drawn to an even earlier settlement (La Posta) at this site going back to the 1820s. Americans came to Cabezon during the 1880s. The San José Church (1890s) commands attention along with a few other structures built several years later. In fact, the 1969 mega-hit *Easy Rider* opened with a scene shot on Cabezon's deserted street. The ghost town (private), abandoned during the 1930s because of dust and then regional flooding, is only slightly visible behind a locked gate; crane your neck and holler for the caretaker. Or, return to the main road, and continue for some 3/4 of a mile. Veer left where you see the post, marked BLM 1114. After another 3/4 mile, you'll get a second chance to view Cabezon off to your left side. Incidentally, there's a slippery but intriguing hiking trail up to Cabezon Peak, found further down this route, past the wash. The last time I checked, however, portions of the surrounding area appeared to be closed off temporarily as part of a wildlife study. The Bureau of Land Management (761-8768) maintains the juniper and aster-studded rocky trail. Contact the BLM for the status of this hike and the exact location of its current access spot.

To the southwest of Cuba, you'll find byways leading to points of interest. Cruise NM 197; at 4.25 miles, you'll spy a gate to the right. Geology fans should rove the dirt track that approaches the mesa, the site of petrified wood specimens. The Johnson Trading Post lies further down NM 197, roughly 15 miles from Cuba, as you enter Navajo-owned lands. One will run across Torreon (26 miles in) where NM 197 becomes Rte. 9, a ranching village containing the remains of a little pueblo. A Chaco outlier was once excavated at Pueblo Pintado (turn right on a dirt track after the twin water towers and go 1/4 mile), which shows up fifty-six miles from Cuba, and the trading post (655-3310) here deals in a pile of pelts, baskets, and old pawn. Some of the best items are in the vault.

A notable archeological site, the Nogales Cliff House of the Gallina Culture (1100-1300 AD), can be discovered to the north of Cuba. To reach this locale, go four miles past Cuba, take a right onto Route 96, and proceed some thirteen miles, bypassing Regina. (A sign for the San José Trail, by the way, should pop up at about the eight-mile point on the east side.) Then follow Route 112 for eleven miles, just beyond Llaves. Forest Road 313 should be visible to the left. Drive F.R. 313 for a short distance passing most of the oil tanks, over a cattle guard and around a yellow-painted hunk of metal fence. Make a right onto a side access, at the yellow "stick," where there's a small pump alongside an informal parking turnout. From here, the road into the forest (the one that goes straight, since the road to the left swoops back to 313) deteriorates into a deeply rutted track, best handled by a high clearance vehicle. If you're in a passenger car, you might have to walk this stretch (maybe 30-40 minutes on foot). One crosses another cattle guard near a wooden fence and storage hut, eventually reaching a tin shed, where you turn left. You'll head towards the base of the cliff (west), and then a little to the right (north), to catch sight of the trailhead close to a wash. The trail is steep in places. Allow perhaps 40 minutes to an hour. Shelters tucked into the rocky escarpments of the Southwest were usually placed there for defensive reasons, as newcomers (forebears of the Navajo) charged down from the Four Corners a century or two after the demise of Chaco Canyon. Archeologists also believe that Chaco survivors harassed the existing highland peoples of this immediate vicinity a bit earlier. Local clans began to fight each other over threatened or shrinking territory. Whatever the motive, postholes, which imply stockades (and nervous residents), have been unearthed nearby, scraped out of solid sandstone, while decapitated skeletons have been uncovered in the general region around Lindrith, where settlements were looted or burned. This particular cliff house has been designated as a Heritage Resource site. Two levels of adobe rooms are wedged into a cave at an altitude of 7800 ft..

The San Pedro Wilderness is one of the two most important recreational resources near Cuba. About 41,000 acres in size, the San Pedro Park (set aside in the 1940s) is a high plateau averaging 10,000 ft. in elevation. San Pedro Peak reaches 10,577 ft., and Nacimiento Peak, just west of San Gregorio Lake, climbs to 9761 ft.. The Nacimiento Mountains blend into the San Pedro Mountains, which become the backdoor of the Jemez Mountains as you move southeast. Damp granitic soils produce very dense stands of conifers, spruce, and aspen, laced with wet meadows. Call the Cuba Ranger Station (289-3264) of the Santa Fe National Forest for info on the Vacas and other trails, or on camping. Camping at the designated campgrounds costs $5 per night, but primitive sites may be more available during non-drought times (when fire restrictions are looser). These areas are best approached in late spring through mid-autumn. For a pleasant outing, drive east out of Cuba on 126 through a beautiful canyon. The aspen and oak put on a stunning show of yellow to honey gold shades during fall. This road is paved for ten miles. You should then hit the can't-miss sign that says San Gregorio Lake. Go left here on Forest Road 70. Park at the lot for Trail 51, located at the three-mile point. The easy-to-follow hike to the reservoir is 1 3/4 miles long, and it will take you about 40-50 minutes to get to this luxuriant setting moving at a moderate pace. Mountain Bluebells and orangey-colored Indian

On Highway 126 near Cuba

paintbrush are two of the common wildflowers that peep up through the thick undergrowth in summer. The lake, which sits at an elevation of 9400 ft., is dammed at one end but can be circumnavigated, if you are willing to trek through a pot-holed area. Along the dam itself, people collect wild raspberries. Other trails thread out from the north side of the San Gregorio Reservoir, or are accessible by driving further up Forest Road 70. The parking area for Trail 50 awaits 7 miles further along, and this path also swivels through the forest.

If you return to 126 and continue east, you run into some wonderful high country of lazy fields and abundant woodland. Families of wild turkey frequently strut through the grass. A couple of summer homes and ranches resemble calendar photos set in green glens along this washboardy route. Though the road is unpaved, a regular sedan can make it in dry weather, but avoid the winter snow pack (126 is blocked off part of the year). Clear Creek Campground crops up a mile after the pavement ends, while the Rio de las Vacas Campground appears a mile later. A sidetrack to Rock Creek Mesa bends to the left at the four-mile point. A convenient turnaround emerges in eight more miles. All in all, the dirt portion of Road 126, also called the Jemez Trail, dips and climbs for nineteen miles to the state park. Road 126 then becomes asphalt again soon after Fenton Lake Park (treated in the Jemez Springs chapter). There is at least one hostelry on the way into Jemez Springs, where you can choose to end this loop.

The other outstanding attraction near Cuba is Chaco Canyon (managed by the National Park Service; 786-7014), the most famous prehistoric site in New Mexico and one of the better-known complexes in the United States. Chaco Canyon reposes between low mesas and is covered with brushy shrubs, as hawks sail overhead. The canyon is not the most scenically magnificent in New Mexico, but the consolidated Anasazi villages, dating to the era of the 900s-1200s AD, are in a comparatively remarkable state of preservation. The general term Anasazi is used to represent prehistoric peoples from the northern half of the state. There are a series of smaller ruins as well as larger ones. Peak occupation occurred during the 1000s to the 1100s or so, eventually eclipsed by drought. Much of the state's prehistory is written from the perspective of Chaco's dramatic rise and fall. The villagers ultimately shifted to other locations throughout the Santa Fe region and along the Rio Grande. The Chaco turnoff comes up 50 miles north of Cuba, indicated by a small sign on the left (west). There are a couple of gas stations on the way, one of which is quite close to where you will leave Hwy. 550 (that is, old Hwy. 44). From here, one must drive a tad over 20 miles more (some 16 are washboard), a rough but clearly marked route. This is Navajo country, and remote. Don't be surprised to see sheep or the occasional hogan (eight-sided ceremonial hut). A mile beyond the park entrance, the RV loop materializes to the right. The campground (ok for tents) offers toilets, but no shower facilities, supplies, or shade, so bring your own stuff; this is a frigid place in winter and hot in summer. Non-windy spring days and fall are the best times. Some ninety thousand people come here annually, and visitation swells on Memorial Day and July 4. You can park at the visitor center in order to buy a pass ($8 per person), see a video, purchase books, or inquire about evening lectures. The trails to various sites close at dusk. A small observatory provides a fine view of the dazzling night sky.

The park is organized such that automobiles drive around an oblong circuit to a handful of sites. The area, which may have supported a populace of several thousand, looks dry now. It's hard to imagine prosperous communities here, but Chaco Wash, and regional rainfall, could have been more dependable water sources hundreds of years ago. Though some sections

South Gap and Chaco Wash from Pueblo Bonito

have been compromised, the relative isolation of Chaco probably saved it from more serious impact. Many of the remains were created from native sandstone, which survived the ages, whereas adobe pueblos tended to melt away. In fact, some of the veneered masonry is striking both for its solidity as well as for its exceptional visual appeal. The first major ruin is Hungo Pavi, lived in from 1000-1250 AD. Chetro Ketl is next, begun about 1020. This "great house" eventually reached 500 rooms in size, and the overall ground plan was a "D" shape. Watch for the glass-fronted door that protects decorative mural fragments.

Pueblo Bonito, the most renowned complex, files in last, constructed over phases from 850-1150 and, at one time, four stories in height. There aren't many places in the U.S. where you can stand in a room almost a thousand years old. You will pass core and veneer walls, made from stones that were faced with thoughtfully chosen surfacing fragments. As one climbs the short trail, the weekend traveler will gain an inspiring vantage point of the town layout and numerous huge kivas, built in sequences that were evidently carefully planned. Only several hundred people resided in Pueblo Bonito at any given time, since dozens of satellite communities, spread around northern New Mexico and occupied seasonally, contributed crops or labor to the main effort at Chaco. The precise level of political organization is debatable. Logs were used to roof these structures. Bits of turquoise and shell found in burials point to a broad trade system. A type of white-slipped pottery that originated at Chaco was in turn distributed or mimicked over a vast region. A couple of corner openings are interpreted as "solstice windows" that may have signaled key moments in the agricultural cycle, while other openings might be related to phases of the moon.

Myriad theories have been advanced about Chaco. A few of them are recycled periodically. Experiments were once conducted that show certain structures within the villages had line-of-sight alignments, handy for communication with flares over an enormous area. Another recent theory has used the evidence of human teeth marks on bones to indicate cannibalism as a lifestyle regimen! Perhaps this was a desperate response to climatic disaster. The large plaza at Pueblo Bonito, on the other hand, would have been ideal for major functions involving lots of people during Chaco's thriving periods. Frankly, despite decades of work and solid scholarship, there is still a good deal of speculation about Chaco Canyon, and many unknowns, and controversy. Note that it's possible to take a tour with a ranger by making arrangements at the visitor center.

Several trails are available within Chaco Canyon. For example, the 6.4-mile (roundtrip) Peñasco Blanco Trail follows Chaco Wash off to the west beyond Pueblo Bonito; you can do an about-face near the halfway point, past the Kin Kletso site (ca. 1125 AD), in order to backtrack from the remains of Casa Chiquita. Petroglyphs line this route. Moreover the Wijiji trailhead will be observed on the way out, a 1.5-mile walk (one-way) to some symmetrical ruins dated to about 1100 AD. Ask at the visitor center for other ideas. Be forewarned that sturdy shoes are a wise bet, and bring a canteen.

Chimayo

Population: 1,500
Elevation: 6500 ft.
Distance from Albuquerque: 89 miles

Chimayo may seem removed from the American mainstream, even now. The drive to Chimayo up I-25 and Hwy. 285 is not especially inspiring, however, because of the ever-increasing commuter traffic to and from Santa Fe. A Santa Fe bypass has facilitated movement up to a point. Otherwise follow the 285 signs along St. Francis Drive. Or, you might take North 14. An interstate exit immediately past Santa Fe hooks up with County Roads 850, and then 590, skirting snugly between the city center and the mountains, headed north through Tesuque Pueblo. El Nido (corner Bishops Lodge Rd. and 590) is an upscale café, once a bordello, which could appear at the right moment some evening. Any way you go, try to maneuver between rush hours, and, during hot weather, remember that morning travel is preferable.

Today's interstate is not far from earlier trails that wound close to the pueblos of the Rio Grande. The high desert phases out past Albuquerque as you forsake the lower river, or Rio Abajo, for the upper Rio Grande region, called the Rio Arriba, beyond La Bajada Mesa. After Santa Fe, juniper-covered hills twist into clumps of red sandstone badlands crisscrossing Pojoaque and Nambe reservations. The orchards and fields of narrow but fertile valleys were inhabited by prehistoric peoples way before Spanish colonial farmers established their homesteads here. The surviving eight northern pueblos spread to the other side of Santa Fe, tapering off at Taos. You'll get off of Hwy. 285 at Pojoaque, as Route 503 veers to the right, embracing you in a canopy of trees and jacal or coyote fences. The Rio Grande transforms into a skinny brown band squeezed by a gorge north of its confluence with the Chama River. The sierras of New Mexico attain some of their highest elevations in this region, the Sangre de Cristos forming the spectacular backdrop for several spots on the map. No less than four peaks are named for the town of Truchas. These run to the east of that village, South Truchas reaching 13,103 ft., the third tallest mountain in the state. Ponderosa pine and meadows fringe Hwy. 76 as one climbs into the high country.

General

Chimayo is one of those touchstones that people visit when they first move to New Mexico, or maybe take their friends and relatives to on a day trip. Yet the area deserves a closer inspection, not just because of the acclaimed Santuario, but because there are several things to check out in this intensely historical portion of the state. San Juan and San Gabriel (once just north of Española around San Juan Pueblo and Chamita) were the first two settlements "founded" by Europeans during the last gasp of the 1500s, on opposite sides of the Rio Grande. In reality, these locations were Indian villages taken over by the Spaniards for several years. Even so, the incursion was the second permanent European colonization in the United States. Spanish people filtered into the Santa Cruz valley throughout the seventeenth century. Their farms and ranches were smashed during the Pueblo Revolt, but they returned, setting up Santa Cruz de la Cañada with Santa Fe migrants, a fair portion of whom were from Zacatecas, Mexico. Chimayo, situated atop a Tewa community, may have coalesced informally during 1692-1693 as an *español* and native refugee encampment after skirmishes inflamed by the reconquest. Some 71 families were recorded here in 1776. Truchas (ca.1754) and other nearby towns made their debut during the eighteenth century.

The region north of Santa Fe is still heavily Hispanic. Many traditions prevail. Archaic New Mexican Spanish hangs by a thread, a leftover from the time of Cervantes. When famed friar Atanasio Domínguez arrived in New Mexico as the American Declaration of Independence was being signed, he found the Spanish of the locals to be already dated and difficult to understand! But old Spanish is currently under pressure from Mexican Spanish, and from English, as well as from television and out-migration. On the other hand, several Indian Pueblos, verging towards extinction by the early 1900s, have revived, opening accommodations, casinos, and museums. There are a couple of colonial churches, lakes, pueblos, waterfalls, cultural facilities, and dramatic green valleys that are good to explore and muse upon, once you leave the mayhem of Hwy. 285 behind.

Practicalities

The vicinity offers only a few places to stay, though there is a hotel. Several alternatives boast definite charm. Pojoaque Pueblo (455-0515; $75-95 range but depends on season; intersection of Hwy. 285 and 502 on east side) operates a full service hotel of 130 rooms, furnished in Mexican as well as southwestern décor, with finishing touches created by local native artisans. Chimayo itself is becoming a mini-mecca for bed and breakfasts. Casa Escondida (351-4805; $80-140 range; just off Hwy. 76) keeps eight rooms with private baths, some with kitchenettes; look for slightly lower rates in winter. Hacienda Rancho de Chimayo (351-2222; $75-115 range; Country Road 98 across from restaurant) is in the century-old adobe home of the Jaramillo family, featuring antiques, fireplaces, and private baths encircling a rambling courtyard. An apple orchard hems the property, open to guests since the 1980s. Rancho Manzana (351-2227; $98-115 range; TaosWebb.com) has adobe rooms with fireplaces plus a hot tub. This luxurious inn is situated within the colonial residence and mercantile store of the Ortega family, and the staff cooks up a hearty breakfast. La Posada de Chimayo (351-4605; $400-800 range per week) maintains vacation rental guesthouses with fireplaces and fully-equipped kitchens. Meson de la Centinela (351-2280; $80-95 range) manages three cozy casitas containing kitchenettes, patios, and fireplaces within the interesting setting of a horse and donkey ranch. Ask for a tour of the little foundry.

The Rancho Arriba in nearby Truchas (689-2374) purveys three rooms in the seventy-dollar range, while Truchas Farmhouse (689-2245) has opened guest lodgings as well. One can also bail out and stay in Española, should you lose your shirt at a casino and decide to save a few pesos. Chain motels (Super 8, Days Inn, etc., in the $50-80 range, depending on season) proliferate on 285, south of the junction with State Road 68, which heads northeast. Comfort Inn provides an indoor pool. The chains have made it tough for the local entries to survive. El Ranchero

(1704 N. Riverside Dr.; $30 range) represents a rock bottom budget choice on the north side of town up the street from Walmart. The Travelers Motel is within a few blocks on the east side of the main drag.

You would be wise to bring your own provisions to the places with individual-suite kitchen facilities. The hotel at Pojoaque does have a restaurant, open for breakfast and dinner, not to mention a luncheon buffet at the casino, which sits across from the hotel guest parking lot. Rancho de Chimayo (County Road 98; usually open daily from 12-9; recommended; moderate) should not be missed, an atmospheric adobe restaurant and patio whipping up traditional dishes like flautas covered with locally grown red chile. Chimayo's red chile is well regarded throughout the state and can be found occasionally in Albuquerque supermarkets. Leona's operates next to the Santuario, while the Milagro Café faces the Santo Niño Chapel.

Española of course supplies fast food, cafes, and a couple of better restaurants. El Paragua's spicy fare (603 Santa Cruz Rd., on NM 76 at Hwy. 68 intersection; moderate to expensive) remains handy to a visit to Santa Cruz. This establishment has been in business since the 1960s with a loyal following, and an ancient cottonwood literally grows out of the bar. Anthony's on the Delta (228 Paseo del Oñate, as Hwy. 84 veers northwest towards Chama; 753-4511; open 5-9; bar service) is located in an adobe manse accented with hand-carved wooden details. Flavio's opens for breakfast and lunch, except Saturdays, and advertises vegetarian entrees (230 Paseo del Oñate). The Four Winds Restaurant and Gallery (open 11:30 am-9 pm; 747-2700) appears a few miles west of Chimayo on Hwy. 76. Los Arcos (819 N. Riverside; 753-3015) constitutes a trendy, fairly new entry in Española turning out traditional cuisine.

Things to do

Chimayo is a delightful place to walk around, since it nestles around a small plaza of sorts (the Plaza del Cerro), a stream, and a couple of winding lanes, honeycombed with historical buildings. The town has been relatively secluded until modern times, and its surrounding hills were considered protection against winter storms, affording a fine fruit harvest. Chile peppers and flowers adorn the adobes enfolded by greenery. Indians were resettled in the vicinity after the Pueblo Revolt. So it's possible that a major church dedi-

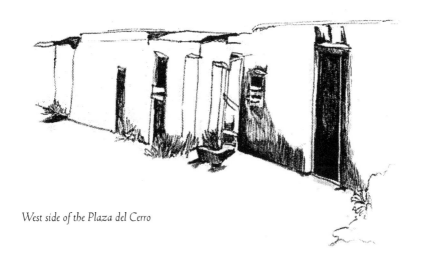

West side of the Plaza del Cerro

cated to St. Bonaventure was put up at the end of the 1600s, but if so, the structure was gone when mapmakers surveyed this area in 1779. Or, this edifice might be confused with a local oratorio (private chapel) that was dedicated to St. Bonaventure, built by the Ortega family in the early 1700s. It seems that the name of the oratorio became synonymous with the place for a time. A defensible plaza was set up by the 1740s, even as verdant ranchos sprouted along the river throughout the eighteenth century. In 1805, the Bazan brothers, master weavers from Spain, were imported into Santa Fe to revive a dying tradition. They soon relocated to lovely Chimayo, initiating a strong crafts movement. Embroideries, carpeting, woolen cloth, and stockings were being woven here on a noticeable scale, as the first quarter of the nineteenth century progressed.

Local craftsmen continue to work on hand-made looms, and you can talk to them at several shops. Ortega's Weaving Studio and Gallery (County Road 98 at Hwy. 76) is a good place to sample some eight generations of textile artistry. The rugs, blankets, vests, and coats are a testament to an enduring mainstay. A tiny museum stands behind Ortega's, and the Casa Feliz Gift Shop is but a few doors away. Trujillo's (.7 miles west on NM 76) has been around for some years. The Chimayo Trading and Mercantile (further west on Hwy. 76) showcases the output of American, Hispano, and

Native American artists, and it's easy to visit, as the store is open seven days a week. There's an RV campground in back.

In the beginning of the nineteenth century, local citizen Bernardo Abeyta constructed the Santuario de Chimayo (351-4889; open daily 9-5, southeast end of town). A new gravel parking area sprawls just before the village. Abeyta's chapel served as a thanksgiving for his relative prosperity, and more importantly, he was cured of an illness after having touched the earth at a tiny spring here. The church is dedicated to Nuestro Señor de Esquípulas. One story discloses that two priests were martyred at this spot, which eventually resulted in Abeyta having a vision. Whatever the reason, the floor of the nave (or main section) was dug from the hillside. The church measured sixty feet long with massive walls some three feet thick, finished in 1816. The Santuario had 38 large bultos (holy statues), a zaguán (carriage entrance), and an adjacent parochial school. The standing narthex (a vestibule or entrance room leading to the nave of the church) is unusual in New Mexico churches. Over the years, streams of pilgrims have come from Colorado to Chihuahua, leaving their crutches and bandages behind upon massaging their afflicted parts with Santuario soil, found in the anteroom behind the altar. A tea made from Chimayo soil was claimed to be even more powerful. The faithful likewise say that one could throw a tad of this dirt into a storm to change its direction. The "miraculous" earth pit has been refilled many times. Nevertheless, tens of thousands of folks make a pilgrimage to Chimayo's church every Good Friday, and healings still occur once in a while. Other stories declare that Chimayo's large crucifix over the altar, sent to different locations during various crises, has mysteriously reappeared more than once. The corbelled-ceiling interior will seem dark and otherworldly on a sunny day.

The controversial Penitente Brotherhood is associated with Chimayo because of Easter. New Mexico's Franciscan missionaries used to act out the Way of the Cross, or Christ's journey to Calvary, at this time. A lay organization called the Penitentes (or more properly, Cofradia, a mutual aid society in times of sickness) took over the ceremony after the Franciscans were ousted during the 1700s. Scholars dispute the date and exact circumstances of the group's emergence. This male confraternity, important to the social and spiritual life of a backwater colony, may have been influenced by medieval customs carried over from the Old World, when self-flagellation was not unusual. Many Spanish communities, particularly in the more remote northern part of the state, chose a Penitente member to participate in a symbolic reenactment of the Crucifixion. A lay brother was actually tied on a cross with horsehair ropes for several minutes. Although warned about extremism, the Church acknowledged this secret society during the

Territorial entryway in the Plaza del Cerro

twentieth century. Penitente brothers and others sometimes carry enormous crosses to Chimayo during Holy Week.

A private chapel (ca. 1856) dedicated to El Santo Niño, or the Holy Child, is also open to visitors 9-6 in summer, and 9-4 at other times, a few steps past the Santuario on Santo Niño Drive. This structure was taken over by the Archdiocese of Santa Fe in 1992. Curative events have been linked to the little statue, which may be covered with prayers written on tiny pieces of paper. The wooden floors creak as you walk in. The St. Bonaventure Oratorio also stands within several hundred yards of the Ortega Shops (ask at Ortega's for the precise location). Residents believe it was built around 1710-15.

East of Chimayo, you'll encounter some old villages. Cordova is a tiny hamlet on Hwy. 76 that has resisted the Anglo world despite many serious changes and challenges. You probably won't find Cordova described at length by the auto club, although these craftsmen have been noted for their weaving, but more especially, for their outstanding woodworking, from sculpture to furnishings. Popular subjects have included birds, carts carrying the icon of death, and the nativity of Christ. The most well known carver of the area,

José Dolores López, once created a famous unpainted cross, decorated with stars and "diamonds," the plain wood being his trademark. Unfortunately, the cross was stolen. Nonetheless, descendants of the López family and others participate in this traditional cottage industry, indicated by the signs in front of several houses. St. Anthony Church was in use by the 1830s, built originally as a private chapel. You may have to rouse the postmaster in order to get inside, but the altar screen images were probably painted between 1834 and 1838, with a couple from the 1860s.

A little further up Hwy. 76, Truchas (meaning trout) got going during the mid-1700s, and in some ways, it may seem as though the place hasn't changed much. Comanche raids pummeled the village, along with rest of New Mexico, during the 1770s, when Truchas had a population of 120 people. The church was apparently revamped by the mid-1800s. In *Red Sky at Morning*, Richard Bradbury described the mountain air of Truchas as joyous to breathe. Tin roofs arise from several bean fields at an elevation of 8,000 ft.. Dancer Martha Graham loved this area so much that she had her ashes spread here. Moreover, Robert Redford shot the *The Milagro Beanfield War* in Truchas during the later1980s, based on the novel by John Nichols, after Chimayo refused the intrusion. The dusty roads and toppling adobe houses of Truchas (population 650) proved to be an evocative setting for the story based on the fragmentation of traditional farm and sheep lands. Outsiders (developers, government agencies, and Anglo ranchers) have helped to break up Spanish land grants in this region by circumventing the property rights of locals in American courts. People without adequate acreage find it tough to make a living from the land, so the residents find scant jobs or leave. Yet though barbed wire has replaced wattle fences, somehow these mountain towns manage. Reduced grazing has resulted in the hillsides becoming green again, giving birth to a network of trails that trickle into Carson National Forest. Truchas appears to be turning into a budding arts center with weaving and woodcutting shops, a couple of families making their mark in the textile business. The Hand Artes Gallery displays folk crafts. One or two cafes have opened.

Seven miles west of Chimayo on NM 76, Santa Cruz merits a stop if you are interested in southwest historic settlements. This is one site that was never really a mission. New Mexico's distinguished Governor Diego de Vargas mustered pack mules in Santa Fe to assist the folks who were sent up in the spring of 1695. These new people may have resided more on the north bank of the Santa Cruz River than had the earlier pioneers from the 1600s. There were 100 families counted in Santa Cruz by the mid-1700s. In fact, the larger valley and northern villages eventually encompassed the heftiest portion of New Mexico's late colonial populace. The church, paid for by the citizenry, was constructed between 1733-48. It's one of the largest in

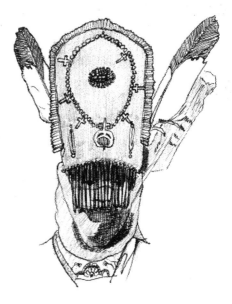

San Juan Matachines dancer

the state. "New" roofs were added during the 1780s and early 1900s. Go inside to see the pine floors, recently varnished, and outstanding religious art consisting of Spanish and Mexican paintings. One can purchase a picture of the wonderful retablo over the altar (*retablos* are paintings on wood slabs). The Iglesia de Santa Cruz poses, along with several old adobes, on the lopsided informal plaza (just up Route 583), which now functions more and more as a suburb of Española. Communities were supposed to be organized around central squares according to Iberian ideas of city planning, though in reality, this arrangement did not always materialize. Santa Cruz de la Cañada was one of only four formally recognized Hispanic townships in New Mexico during the early eighteenth century.

San Juan (852-4400; hotel at 753-5067), the largest Tewa pueblo at over a couple of thousand inhabitants, was known as Ohkay when Don Juan de Oñate plopped down here with several hundred soldiers, friars, and camp following wives in 1598. To get to San Juan, head north on NM 68 for three miles (from the Hwy. 76 intersection), and then west for a mile. The Spaniards brought an incredible amount of baggage with them transported in dozens of carts. The colonists were prepared for a long stay, but after a year or so, they moved to the other side of the Rio Grande. Nevertheless, the name they chose for this location—San Juan de los Caballeros (St. John of the Gentlemen)—stuck. The newcomers built a short-lived chapel when they arrived. By the 1770s, there was a substantial church described as being 100 feet long with a ceiling supported by forty corbeled beams. The current stone chapel harkens to about 1890, resting near two older (and very non-public) kivas, a rather common and perhaps suggestive arrangement. The brick church (ca. 1912) replaced the "unfashionable" colonial structure of adobe, which was deliberately dynamited by the fathers! A respected crafts cooperative, open six days a week with design displays, sits adjacent, where you could find traditional seed necklaces. It was a resident of San Juan Pueblo called Popé who masterminded the Pueblo Revolt of 1680 and even now, San Juan plays a central role in native affairs, housing the headquarters of the Eight Northern Pueblos Indian Council. Farming, buffalo raising, and a budding arts program are supplemented by a hotel, casino, restaurant, and RV park as tribal activities. These facilities spill along Hwy. 68. A fishing pond exists on site. The feast days are June 23-24 (St. John's Day), commemorated with Buffalo Dances, and June 13 (St. Anthony's Day). Performance rituals also occur on Christmas and January 6, starting very roughly at 10 am. One might see the yuletide Matachines Dance, rooted in the Christian victory over the Moors, a breath-taking spectacle wherein participants don "bishop's mitre" hats wildly spangled with ribbons or turquoise.

Santa Clara (753-7330; 753-7326) is the other big Tewa-speaking community (almost two thousand people), and these folks maintain a visitor center. The village is located just a couple of miles to the southwest of Española on Route 30. Follow 84-285 as it veers northwest, and look for the sign to Route 30 on the left, headed southward. One church (the town's third) was begun in 1758, when the pueblo contained 67 families; the building was supplanted by a small structure in 1918, now partly renovated. Residents are known for their black as well as red pottery, which may be intricately incised (called sgraffito). A shop sells ceramics and sculpture, the now famed "wedding vase" form often attributed to Santa Clara or Acoma potters. Still, Santa Clara suffered from a lot of internal strife during the early 1900s as the two principal social divisions, the Summer and Winter moieties, clashed

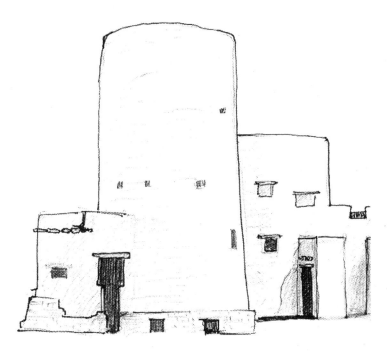

Poeh Center and Museum

over priorities, resulting in a constitution by the 1930s. The act became, in a sense, the springboard of a modern stab at self-sufficiency. This group is opening a casino (Big Rock) and movie theatre in Española. If you prefer a taste of sweeping landscapes and the distant past, visit the 700-year-old Puye Cliff Dwellings, joined by two levels of ladders and stairways carved into volcanic tuff cliffs. Here the reservation unfolds into peaks, working farms, pumice quarries, grasslands, and valleys, the Tewa name of Kha P'o meaning "Valley of the Wild Roses." Drive south of the village for three miles and then west on 601, a.k.a. Route 5, for seven miles. Watch for developed campsites here, about to reopen after a fire (call for permit info). Ancestors of the contemporary pueblo lived in caves along Santa Clara Canyon until drought forced them closer to the river six centuries ago. Santa Clara celebrates feast days for its patron saint on August 12 and for St Anthony on June 13, with more dances at Christmas.

South of Chimayo, Pojoaque Pueblo (455-3460; population 130) straddles the Los Alamos to Santa Fe route, with a tourist center and other facilities on the east side of 285. Pojoaque has long been the smallest of the Tewa pueblos. The place was occupied during the time of Oñate in the sixteenth century, but deserted after 1680, to be reestablished by the Spanish governor in 1706. Some 79 souls lived here in 1712, a number that rose to 368 by 1788. Then disease struck. Eventually the population escalated once more, but as late as World War I, Pojoaque practically disappeared due to a smallpox epidemic. Many moved into other native communities or even Santa Fe, evidently merging with the locals. Not much remained of the original town. Yet in a landmark decision, federal legislation reorganized and protected native lands as of the 1930s, and key residents returned. Though the current village is not exactly idyllic, these people have bounced back like the proverbial phoenix. A shopping center has been developed and an industrial park planned. The Poeh Arts Program teaches pottery and sculpture to tribal members. The Poeh Cultural Center and Museum (closed Sun.-Mon.; 455-2489), built in the style of ancestral pueblos, houses traditional objects and the work of hundreds of artists to constitute one of the larger selections of native crafts in the state. Watch for dancing demonstrations here in summer. On the flip side of the activity spectrum, the Cities of Gold Casino (once the high school) provides 40,000 square feet of risk. If you ever craved the sound of 700 clinking slot machines, this is your chance. These folks acquired Santa Fe Downs several years ago, seat of the Indian Nations Futurity cup, while Pojoaque Enterprises has also opened a pizza parlor and a sports bar in case you overdose on quiet. Pojoaque's dancers can be seen on December 12, the feast day of Our Lady of Guadalupe.

Nambe Pueblo (455-2036; population 500) is another of the six Tewa-speaking native hamlets of northern New Mexico. This attractive reservation of 19,000 acres skirts the Santa Fe National Forest and Sangre de Cristo Range. The general locale has been inhabited for several hundred years, perhaps as far back as the 1300s. The small village emerges a little over a mile from NM 503 along Route 101. While the Franciscans started one church here dedicated to St. Francis in 1613, it burned during a major rebellion in August of 1680. Disgruntled Nambe residents proceeded to dispatch the next priest, amounting to a second insurrection in 1696. A third or so mis-

Buffalo at Nambe Pueblo

sion structure was begun around 1729, but it collapsed by the early twentieth century. A couple of very old dwellings nonetheless remain. Irrigation
farming continues. A gallery showcases beadwork, contemporary stone sculpture, textured matte ceramics, and a special black and red polychrome pottery made from micaceous clay. Nambe's annual feast day is October 4, a day
dedicated to St. Francis and honored in many places with a Catholic influ-
ence. The July 4 costumed dances may be more popular, though, replete
with food booths plus arts and crafts. (Note: last year the dances were can-
celed. Call to make sure...Nambe has just inaugurated an arts fest in July).
Christmas Eve and Three Kings Day are also important festivals, since the
Animal Dance, which celebrates both antelope and deer, is performed on
January 6. Don't be taken aback by the buffalo. In 1994, the Bison Project
set aside 179 acres devoted to a tribal herd of about 40 animals. Nambe Falls
Lake (455-2304), a 60-acre reservoir amidst juniper uplands at an elevation
of 6700 ft., has a boat ramp, horse trails, and plenty of trout. Drive for five
miles on 101, check in at the ranger booth, and go straight for one more
paved mile; an unpaved route surrounds the lake punctuated by a few picnic
tables. Remember to visit Nambe Falls, fed by the lake and the Rio Nambe.
The waterfall makes a three-tiered plunge, the longest some 100 feet, into
several stone-edged pools. This enticing spot is open from mid-March through

early autumn. From the same ranger booth, take the unpaved .5-mile access to the right. Nambe Falls Campground has hookups for RVs and tent sites ($5 and up), and from here a brief path leads to the cascade, a 10-minute walk. According to one tale, two rival suitors once killed each other, and the maiden who loved them both commenced to cry nonstop, creating the waterfall. Today the falls are considered to be a sacred site, the focus of one or two modern ceremonials.

Santa Cruz Lake National Recreation Site lies several miles south of Chimayo. This pinyon-country retreat in the foothills of the Sangre de Cristos sets forth 120 glimmering surface acres of water at an altitude of 7,000 ft., and is stocked with rainbow trout. Camping (fee $7; drinking water, firepits, and pit toilets on site; 758-8851) is permitted with a fourteen-day limit. The lake, lined with a couple of trails, is popular with fishermen and picnickers. Look for the sign on 503. The weekend traveler must drive a mile over washboard to get to the recreation area, where you run smack into a beautiful overlook. Then the road veers left to reach the lake after .8 mile, a trailhead coming up along on the way. If one resumes NM 503 eastward, the road swirls through miniscule but charming Cundiyo, the home of archaic families, an artist or two, a few horses, and sundry aggressive goats. An orchard grows near the little stream. This place is so out-of-the-way that the post office didn't start six-day delivery here until the 1990s! There's a second lake entrance just before a series of hairpin turns, which signal the upcoming junction with Hwy. 76.

Gallup

Population: 20,000
Elevation: 6510 ft.
Distance from Albuquerque: 137 miles
Chamber of Commerce: (800) 242-4282; 863-3841

Eons ago, when the planet was younger, this portion of the state teemed with life. An immense swamp nurtured a deep jungle of overflowing plants that flourished during the Cretaceous period, a hundred million years in the past. Diverse types of organic debris were slowly pressed together into layers that turned into rich deposits of dark coal. Similarly, the remains of a pinkish desert, not unlike a beach, had its granules cemented into an array of sandstone cliffs near Gallup. The cliffs have often retreated because of erosion, revealing or leaving behind even more beautiful shapes and colors. These formations and coal beds are considered to be part of the Mesaverde Group that outlines the San Juan Basin of northwest New Mexico. This ancient battleground between land and sea dried out as the waters gradually retreated. Later on, as volcanoes thrust towards the sky, peaks and texture were added to the complexion of a developing landscape.

This area is part of a raised platform called the Colorado Plateau. It includes all of the mesas and monoliths of the Four Corners region. Once the home of prehistoric peoples known as the Anasazi, regional inhabitants began to weave baskets and blankets, till cornfields, and dig out pithouses some 1300-1400 years ago. Within two to three more centuries, they constructed multi-room communes close to water sources or on top of escarpments. Some villages were elaborate. Residents came to use imaginatively decorated pottery, grow several types of crops, and trade over very long distances. The Anasazi are gone. Their descendants have dispersed into various pueblos closer to the Rio Grande and its tributaries, or along the Zuni River. The Navajo among others live here now. Where the rivers run are scant verdant fields. Outside of Gallup, there may be as many sheep as people. Flocks graze sections of the high tableland, herded by watchful dogs.

Allow yourself enough time to relinquish the congested world of the interstate for the quiet canyons of uncluttered Amerindian lands. But be prepared for temperature swings that are more dramatic than Albuquerque's. A comfortable day at 80 degrees can turn into a chilly evening of 30 degrees, a fact of interest to campers. And, be wary of driving at night; lots of traffic arrests are made in and around Gallup every year, many of them alcohol related.

General

Gallup sells itself as the gateway to Indian country, which in a way, it is. The town abounds in almost 100 shops that sell Native American crafts. The second largest community in the wide-open spaces of the Four Corners, Gallup is home to more Amerindians than any other major city in the state, with the exception of Albuquerque. Moreover, it's easy to get to the Navajo and Zuni Reservations from here.

Inhabited by indigenous people for thousands of years, the Gallup area once supported at least six Zuni villages when the first Europeans arrived. Today, Zuni Pueblo represents the only place in the United States where the residents speak their own unique language (called, not surprisingly, Zuni), distinct even from other native languages of the Southwest. This feat is astonishing in the age of cultural homogenization, as the media attempt to saturate the landscape of the mind, while corporate America takes over the landscape of the roadway.

Zuni was "discovered" by a black scout, Estevanico, while in the service of Fray Marcos de Niza in 1539. Niza was on an exploratory sojourn at the time, and he sent Estevanico ahead to reconnoiter. The Zunis cut the scout to pieces. Niza was prudently reluctant to move closer, but to him, the Zuni villages appeared, at least at a distance, to be impressive, resembling gold. An avalanche of rumor and speculation followed. Coronado, the first Spanish explorer of interior New Mexico, had hoped to stumble across Niza's purported spectacular golden cities during 1540. Approaching from Arizona, he ran into Hawikuh, now a scant ruin, westernmost and largest of the Zuni adobe-mud towns.

The initial shock and disappointment of the conquistadors wore off during the colonial era as missionaries plied their trade at Zuni Pueblo for many years. Cattlemen and sheep ranchers followed them by the later 1800s, occupying the Gallup region and attracting a stage and Pony Express stop. When the railroad reached the vicinity in 1881, David Gallup was the paymaster of the Atlantic and Pacific Line. The post office simply usurped his name when setting up shop, and the city of Gallup was born. Coal min-

The fabled road

ing and timber cutting stimulated not only an influx of new settlers, but the inevitable rampant prostitution, gambling, and a couple of dozen saloons along with an opera house. The town grew. Gallup was incorporated in 1891. The establishment of the Harvey House Railroad Restaurant during the 1890s brought new respectability to Gallup, not to mention good 75-cent meals, and Gallup became the seat of McKinley County in 1901.

The coal mines operated for several decades, encouraging the construction of brick kilns and other industries. The town served as an important shipping point for Navajo wool clip. Route 66 made its mark here as of the 1920s-1930s, sparking a motel scene that was enhanced when Hollywood discovered western New Mexico. Gallup, a staging point for movies taking advantage of the region's topography, acquired luster as the capital of the B-Western. Billy Wilder's *Big Carnival* starring Kirk Douglas exemplifies a grander project, the story of a man trapped in an Indian ruin! Meanwhile a brother of D.W. Griffith had built the El Rancho Hotel in 1937. The hotel was the biggest and most lavish in this part of the state, overseeing a huge casino that rivaled the waywardness of Las Vegas. Many of the rooms of the El Rancho are still emblazoned with the monikers of the stars who stayed here, a list which includes Humphrey Bogart, Barbara Stanwyck, Katherine Hepburn, Errol Flynn, John Wayne, Spencer Tracy, Robert Mitchum, and

Rita Hayworth. Ronald Reagan slept in Room 103 during the shooting of several episodes of *Death Valley Days* in 1965. The hotel was renovated in the 1980s when purchased by the current owner. It contains plenty of Navajo rugs, rustic wooden accents, and atmospheric esoterica, including the prerequisite elk head.

Eventually the coal mines closed by the 1950s as oil became a more important source of fuel. Since then Gallup has relied on tourism and developing a world market for Indian wares. The demand peaked during the 1970s. Gallup is struggling to boost visitation with events such as a fall film fest.

The Inter-Tribal Indian Ceremonial (1-800-233-4528; 863-3896), *the* major local event since 1922, is held the second week in August, typically starting on a Thursday. Hopi, Navajo, Cheyenne, Kiowa, and Comanche participants, as well as dozens of other groups from as far away as Central America, compete in costumed dancing and trade shows. Attendance has fluctuated back and forth over the years from fifty to thirty-five thousand. Spectators wade through the nine categories of displayed crafts amounting to millions of dollars worth of rugs, beaded dresses, pottery, jewelry, sculpture, and tribal pipes. Perhaps 1,000 artists are represented, and the pricing of objects is generally considered to be reasonable, even wholesale. This is one event that it's ok to photograph, and there are plenty of opportunities, commencing with a big rodeo highlighted by bareback bronco-busting. Parades waft through town on Friday and Saturday. It's a good idea to book in advance if you want to attend.

Practicalities

Gallup is large enough to have maybe 100 places to dine, from fast food to Furr's Cafeteria (up Hwy. 666) to truck stops to Chinese restaurants to sports bars. Though not exactly a gourmet's paradise, you won't go hungry at the roadhouse cafes, which exude a certain Formica allure. On the east side of town, Earl's (1400 E. Hwy. 66; open 7-9 everyday) claims a loyal following devoted to its green chile chicken enchiladas and daily specials. Indian artisans carrying trays of silver rings gad about the tables and pink booths of this highway palace. The Panz Alegra (1201 E. Hwy. 66) is known for Mexican and Italian food plus steaks. Other places crop up a little to the west, closer to Gallup's center. For a Ronald Reagan burger (a bacon cheeseburger with jellybeans on the side), try the El Rancho Hotel at 1000 E. Hwy. 66. The funky Eagle Café (220 W. Hwy. 66; open Mon.-Sat.), possibly the oldest Route 66 diner, dishes up decent ribs or lamb stew. In the heart of downtown, Dominic's (303 W. Coal) is a trendy choice for pizza or sandwiches. Nearby Jerry's (406 W. Coal) caters to a no-nonsense crowd in the mood for burritos. Genaro's Restaurant (600 W. Hill; open Tues.-Sat.) can stuff a mean sopaipilla. Going towards the west end, Don Diego's (801 W. Hwy. 66; open everyday except Sunday) prepares New Mexican food and offers a lounge; Glen's Pastries (9th St. at Route 66) sits across the street, handy for sandwiches or good bakery treats. El Sombrero (1201 W. Hwy. 66) will do take-out as well as breakfast, lunch, or dinner. On the upscale end of the spectrum, Chelles (2201 W. Hwy. 66 by the airport; 722-7698) opens only during the evening. The Ranch Kitchen (3001 W. Hwy. 66; open 7-10 everyday except Christmas and Easter), in business since 1954, serves southwest fare to a solid family clientele, and they will gladly make you a barbeque sandwich or Navajo taco as you select souvenirs at their gift shop. Moving to the town's south side, the Rocket Café (1719 S. Second; open everyday; beer) racks up its share of fans.

Gallup overflows with literally dozens of motels encompassing both the national names and the ultra-budget category. The chains sometimes reduce their rates during winter. Most of these places line up along Hwy. 66, with a couple on Maloney Ave. immediately north of and parallel to the interstate. More or less in the middle, El Rancho (1000 E. Hwy. 66; 863-9311; $55-75 range) definitely has lots of atmosphere. At the west end of town, the Best Western Inn (3009 W. Hwy. 66; 722-2221; $70-110 range; exit 16, then east 1 mile) advertises a garden with fountains and a heated swimming pool. Don't be confused by the fact that Best Western runs two other motels in Gallup. The Red Roof Inn (3304 W. Hwy. 66; 722-7765; $45-70 range) is not far away, whereas the Holiday Inn (2915 W. Hwy. 66; 722-2201; $70 range) sports a game room, heated indoor pool, lounge, and a free hot breakfast. Days Inn Central (1603 W. Hwy. 66; 863-3891; $35-50 range; seasonal pool; exit 20) supplies reasonable rates closer to town. The Golden Desert (1205 W. Hwy. 66; no pets; $20-30 range) represents the super budget category on the west side. Moving to the east end of the highway, the Blue Spruce (1119 E. Hwy. 66; $28-40) is a decent older motor court with economical rates. El Capitan (1300 E. Hwy. 66; 863-6828; $28-40 range) operates adjacent to several restaurants, and the rooms with two beds are comfortably sized. The Roadrunner (3012 E. Hwy 66; 863-3804; $30-40 range; seasonal pool) conveys a twinge of the Route 66 era, this place having the advantage of a small café on the premises. Most of these establishments, particularly the chains in this instance, accept pets either free or for a nominal charge. For a taste of something different, you might want to stay in Zuni Pueblo. The Inn of Halona is a bed and breakfast that has taken over a historical residence and store (23B Pia Mesa Road; 782-4547; $80-90 range). Turn south at the four-way stop on the highway through town and go up a little hill. Stauder's Navajo Lodge (862-7553; about $90) teeters on the Continental Divide, roughly 10 miles west of Thoreau and 20 miles east of Gallup. The Z Lazy-B Guest Ranch (488-5600) roosts near McGaffey Lake at Page. Fully equipped, homey cabins, way up in the mountains and forests some 30 miles southeast of Gallup, cost in the $120 range per night.

Things to do

Gallup contains a fairly concentrated downtown that can be enjoyed by walking. The twelve-block core is bounded by Main St. or Route 66 (north), Fourth St. (west), Hill Ave. (south), and First St. (east). Coal Ave. lies just to the south of Main. The former Rex Hotel (300 W. Route 66) dates from about 1900. Other historical hotels include the boarded-up Grand Hotel at 306 West Coal and the Lexington (408 W. Hwy. 66). The Lexington, some 12,000 square feet in size, is in the process of undergoing renovation. Built in 1931, it holds murals painted by artist Carl Van Hassler. El Morro Theatre (207 W. Coal) presents a lively facade in the exaggerated grandeur of super-eclectic Colonial Revival. The McKinley County Courthouse (201 W. Hill), a good example of Pueblo Revival, was constructed in 1938 and decorated inside with a mural; watch for art shows here. Downtown also has many of the city's trading posts, galleries, and turn-of-the-century buildings. Trading posts originated during the later 1800s on reservation lands. The phrase was retained in the twentieth century because of its romantic appeal, and the Gallup area has more of these places than anywhere else in the state. Richardson's Trading Post and Pawn (222 W. Hwy. 66) has been in business since 1913 with kaleidoscopic displays in its big storefront window. Bill

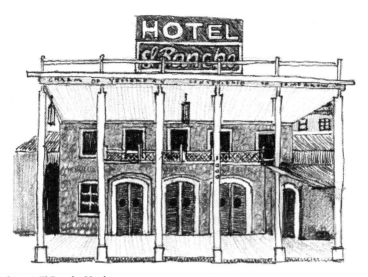

The historic El Rancho Hotel

Richardson can glimpse at a piece of Indian jewelry and tell you where the turquoise came from and what it's worth. Tobe Turpen's (1710 S. Second), another retailer dealing in Indian and Western collectibles, has been around since the 1920s; formerly part of the Hubbell fiefdom, the structure still exhibits a tin ceiling and old bullpen. Back downtown, the Navajo Trading Co. (232 W. Hwy. 66) maintains its devotees. The City Electric Shoe Shop (230 W. Coal), founded in 1924, sells all sorts of interesting leather merchandise spanning cowboy boots to moccasins to saddles. A new arts cooperative, the Silver Bear Gallery (233 W. Coal), specializes in Zuni items. In addition, downtown features the antiquated train station, constructed by the Santa Fe Railroad in 1916 (now the Cultural Center at 201 E. Hwy. 66). Flavorful cottages, some derelict and some rehabilitated, encircle the core. The obsessed should check out the other stores that extend to the west and east of the city's central portion.

And don't dismiss the pawnshops. They often stock authentic squash blossom necklaces (derived from the crescent and pomegranate motifs in Spanish-Moorish crafts), wide-cuff Navajo bracelets, or silver horse gear. Someone might pawn a belt buckle in order to pay off a humdrum necessity, like a car note, and then redeem the item later, but a small amount of this merchandise will remain unclaimed, becoming "dead pawn." Something in the possession of the storekeeper for a very long time may have acquired a high value. A bracelet worth $50 in 1930 could ring in at $4,000 today. Be sure and look for the original tag. Totally handmade items are usually older.

Moreover, Gallup is simply a good place to learn a little about Amerindian arts. Navajo jewelry, often chunky with a few massive oval stones, can be contrasted with the colorful, delicate inlay work of the Zuni. Hopi jewelry exhibits silver overlay, or incised patterns in relief, emphasizing the metal rather than the stones. Kachina dolls are also popular. Kachina dolls portray the kachina dancers of Pueblo ceremonials, where the performers in turn impersonate supernatural beings, from mountain lions to colorful ogres. There are well over 200 different types. Navajo rugs, which have creative roots in the colonial era (when the Navajos swiped sheep from the Spaniards and adopted Puebloan weaving techniques), started to move into the general marketplace, as with jewelry, by roughly the 1880s. Heavier and better wools were developed, and regional styles appeared. Black, white, red, and gray tones were supplemented by browns and other vegetal dyes a few decades ago. Beware that an authentic rug will have tassels at each corner, but not full end fringe. A rug made on an upright loom will have a dense, durable warp and weft. Monthly auctions at Crownpoint have been taking place since the 1960s, but many rugs are sold through dealers in Gallup. The Best Western (722-6963) way out on West Hwy. 66 hosts an auction each month at 7 pm. These rugs are quite expensive and have a worldwide following. Legend has it that Navajo women, who make these rugs, learned the art of weaving from Spider Woman, a holy personage from the underworld.

If you have questions, the Gallup Visitor's Bureau can sometimes help (863-3841). The nonprofit Indian Arts and Crafts Association (265-9149) is another source. Or, consult a few books and then comparison shop, and ask questions. Note that several of the major outlets have expanded beyond their old downtown locations into the newer commercial hub. The Tanner Family, who accompanied Brigham Young into Utah back in 1847, has been dealing in Indian articles for many years, opening several stores on the Navajo Reservation and in Gallup. The Shush Yaz Trading Co., now located at 1304 W. Lincoln, can be reached by going north on Hwy. 666 (exit 20 if you're approaching from I-40). The Rio West Mall, with 60 stores including chain outlets and trading companies, will be found nearby. It's immediately over the bridge that crosses the interstate from downtown, and then a little to the west, at the corner of NM 666.

The Gallup Cultural Center (201 E. Hwy. 66) is supported by the Southwest Indian Foundation. There's a gallery and small museum devoted to native crafts, local artifacts, and Western memorabilia. This resuscitated building, now owned by Amtrak, offers a café and gift shop. Weekend hours are variable. Indian dancers perform here most evenings throughout the summer, usually starting at 7 pm.

The Rex Museum (corner Third St. and Route 66; 8-4: 30; $2) may be new, but the building is not, a late Victorian hotel conveniently situated next to a parking lot. This facility constitutes a part of Gallup's effort to breathe life into the central city. It's open six days a week. The first floor, a repository for railroad, coalmining, and Route 66 material, conjures up a glance into Gallup's nostalgic past. Red Rock State Park exchanges installations with the Rex Museum from time to time.

The Chamber of Commerce (103 W. Hwy. 66, at the corner of First St.) mounts long-term exhibits on subjects of regional interest. The Navajo Code Talkers are the topic of the current display, open 8: 30-5, Monday through Friday. This group of Native American Marines played an integral part in the Allied victory of World War II. During the years of U.S. involvement in the Pacific theatre, crucial instructions had to be transmitted to wrest various islands from Japanese control. The Japanese could readily break codes in English. But the Navajos, like the Apaches, are an Athabascan-speaking people originally from Canada. These two cultural groups stormed into southwest relatively late (1300 AD?) compared to the Puebloans. Navajo is an extremely complicated language with a unique syntax, ideally suited to intelligence purposes. A group of twenty-nine Navajos devised an unbreakable code, communicating hundreds of error-free messages that led to the critical American victory at Iwo Jima.

Adventures in the vicinity of Gallup

About twenty miles west of Gallup, the weekend traveler will trip across a colossal arching alcove known rather mysteriously as the Cave of the Seven

Devils in Lupton. The Miller Trading Post was begun here in the 1920s. It now carries the name of Chief Yellowhorse. The Chief Yellowhorse Trading Post (exit 8, then eight miles up the service road) is a happy homage to Route 66 with its assortment of both serious and outrageous tourist paraphernalia, from quality jewelry to "faux" tomahawks. A red stripe painted on the floor affords one a singular chance to have one cheek jiggling in New Mexico and the other in Arizona. There are all sorts of residual oddities incorporating make-believe cliff dwellings, innumerable skulls, and buffalo.

A couple of preliminary stops evoke the days when Gallup was known by its alternate handle of Carbon City. Gamerco lingers 2.5 miles north of the interstate up Hwy. 666, past the fast food joints. You'll see the power plant and coal chutes from the region's mining heyday during the 1920s. The Navajo Shopping Center, which pedals car parts to kachinas, has been built just beyond the old mine to the left (west). In fact, the economic focus of Gallup is steadily shifting to the northwest side of town towards the Wal-mart Supercenter. Or, if you head west onto the road north of and paralleling the interstate, and go beyond the hotels, it's easy to find the hamlet of Allison. Look for the stop sign 1.5 miles from Hwy. 666. Hang a right, driving a mile northwest from the intersection up to Coronado Blvd. This tiny Gallup satellite is a relic from the coal mining era with a few buildings from the 1910s-1930s. Allison was so dubbed for one of the principal owners, and it once possessed a populace of close to 500. Today, residents include donkeys, chickens, Chihuahuas, and guinea hens.

The gargantuan Navajo Reservation lies to the north of Gallup. This region could be called the "outback" of the United States, a veritable nation within a nation settled across an exotic landscape. A huge slice of "checkerboard" (non-federal but frequently native owned) Navajo lands skirt the city of Gallup and the east side of Hwy. 371. The federal reservation commences a couple of miles north of Red Rock State Park. It sweeps upward into southern Utah and westward to the Grand Canyon, a sprawling domain of 27,000 square miles, bigger than the state of West Virginia. Some 15 national monuments sit on Navajo soil. The checkerboard and federal portions added together comprise roughly a fourth of the state of New Mexico. Though the Navajo Nation was decimated after the Long Walk of the 1860s (when rounded up by U.S. troops and sent to Fort Sumner), the population has

Navajo Nation Tribal Headquarters / Window Rock, Arizona

rebounded from 8,000 to some 260,000, the largest indigenous group in contemporary America.

The Navajos are not a monolithic society. Some reside and work in Albuquerque, others maintain a modern lifeway within the reservation, and still others manage a "traditional" existence, raising sheep in remote pockets. Cell phone companies are enthusiastically chipping away at this isolation. But almost all the Navajos are considered to be matrilineal, that is, they are organized socially into different clans. A youngster acquires membership through the clan affiliation of his or her mother. Individuals from the same clan cannot marry. Many Navajos even now have a spiritual outlook, believing that one cannot control nature, but must harmonize with it. In fact, some fifty types of ceremonials are practiced, including "sings" to cure the infirmed. Occasionally, one may see a few of the women dressed up in traditional velveteen skirts or blouses, knee-high moccasins, concho belts, and shawls. On the other hand, progressive industry has indelibly touched reservation life since the 1920s. In 1987 alone, some $43 million from mineral royalties and $28 million from coal mining were poured into tribal coffers.

Oil, uranium, vanadium, and gas are significant resources. Folks here are often divided into either pro-development or anti-development camps, the latest flare-up raging over the potential construction of a casino. And, local politics can be pretty dicey because this group is largely self-governing, so various tribal administrations are not without their own juicy scandals from time to time along the lines of Watergate.

A drive up NM 666 into this fascinating region is easy from Gallup. If you have some time on your hands, you might like Todilto Park, an area of sandstone palisades millions of years old. A big part of the following tour, some 24 miles, is unpaved. While a four-wheel drive vehicle is an advantage, residents often tool around this particular route in old sedans. Use your own judgment. Dry conditions, however, are a must. Take a left (west) onto Navajo Route 30 from Hwy. 666, 17 miles north of the interstate. Nakaibito appears quickly (3 miles), a collection of houses and log hogans that draw water from Mexican Spring. The common ending syllable of "to" means spring in Navajo. Years ago, octagonal hogans of earth and timber were furnished in sheepskin beds and wood-burning stoves. Today these structures are relegated to ritual purposes, the people having moved into modern housing. At Nakaibito, Navajo Route 30 becomes a fairly well-maintained washboard road that heads to the left, or west, passing by the chapter house. This track then winds northward along Mexican Wash, lined by majestic cottonwood trees. There are a couple of rough spots and dips; exercise caution, and ignore the sidetracks. Eventually you encounter the foothills of the Chuska Mountains as well as secluded ranches within the emerging forest.

In sixteen miles from Nakaibito, you will hit an "intersection." The route to the right (Navajo 321) leads up to Asaayi Lake in three miles, indicated by a fading sign. You will continue to the left (straight actually but winding westward) on what is now Navajo Route 31 for eight more unpaved miles. As one enters the park, the massive mesas and fierce brick-red colors of the canyon look like Mars. One knobbed protrusion is called Beelzebub, on the south side or left a few miles after the Asaayi turnoff. To your right, you'll see the Venus Needle, a 207-foot tall rock slab that rises some 3 miles before the community of Navajo. The "Beast" is another byproduct of erosion, a crouching, lion-like monster with a 200' face, on the left just before village. These formations are not marked, so use your imagi-

A Navajo hogan

nation. Frog Rock sticks up to the left, visible behind the water tower, as you get ready to rejoin the highway. The microdot of Navajo possesses a sawmill to process timber from the Chuskas. You'll find a gas station and market. Red Lake, immediately north on paved Route 12, bears the ruddy hue of the magnificent cliffs that continue to wear away ever so gradually into this reservoir near the Arizona border. Outlet Neck, a volcanic plug about 100' in elevation, stands at the foot of Red Lake Dam.

You can return to Gallup by trucking south on Rte. 12, even as it jogs once or twice (keep left), to Window Rock. Window Rock is the seat of government on the reservation. If you follow the signs into this village, don't miss the eroded sandstone oval that gives the place its name, near the hogan-style Tribal Council Chamber. Incidentally, the Navajo Nation Inn on eastbound Rte. 264 has a pretty good restaurant. Tony Hillerman's fictional detectives never stop drinking coffee here. The Navajo Nation Museum can be reached on the north side of Rte. 264 right before traversing the New Mexico state line.

Another option is to drive 41 miles past Yah-ta-hey (or 48 miles from Gallup) to Sheep Springs. Sheep Springs owes its existence to its good-tasting waters, and there's a new trading post (replacing an older one next door) along with a handful of homes. From here, a turn west onto paved NM 134 (a.k.a. Route 32) will take you into the Chuskas. This byway crosses over the mountains and links up with Route 12 to swing back to Window Rock (see above). Chuska means white spuce. These mountains, composed of sandstone, shale, and some volcanic ash, are sacred to the Navajo. Eagle feathers are still collected throughout the upper reaches of this range for myriad ceremonials. The ride to Washington Pass, named for a military officer who assembled info on the Navajos in the 1840s, provides breaks in the forest where one gains a terrific viewpoint of the road's climb and the plains below. Crystal, 17 miles from Sheep Springs, is a teeny community with a trading post (ca. 1894) and boarding school, fed by a stream that originates at Washington Pass. Winters at this elevation are decidedly cold. If you hook a left onto unpaved Route 321 (south) at Crystal, you'll reach the Bowl Canyon Recreation Area in 7 miles. A nice spot, Bowl Canyon envelops a lakebed that filled up like a cereal bowl from severe rain in the early 1900s. Asaayi Lake is stocked with catfish. Camp Asaayi features a few rustic cabins for groups only. Individual campsites, on the south side of the lake, are open late spring through very early fall and cost $15 (call the Navajo Parks and Rec. Office at 520-871-6647 for details). Camping and hiking are popular activities.

Some thirty-five miles to the southwest of Gallup, Zuni Pueblo (elevation 6283 ft.; 782-4481; 782-2869) is the largest of the New Mexican native towns with a population of 7,000. Another 2500 people are spread out within the reservation, which amounts to a half-million acres ranging in altitude from 6000 to 8000 ft., edging towards the Zuni Mountains. The Zuni are another matrilineal society organized into various clans (the Turkey clan, etc.). This group believes that their ancestors emerged originally from the Grand Canyon. They were area hunter–gatherers for many centuries before they grew corn along the Zuni River. At present, the Sustainable Agriculture Project is endeavoring to improve farming in the area. These folks also raise livestock. Nevertheless, unemployment is high. The Zunis are famed for their outstanding cottage crafts, this activity accounting for half the income of most households, and jewelry has been a chief mainstay since World War II. The Zunis are justifiably renowned for their inlay work, silversmiths producing compositions of meticulously inlaid pieces of turquoise, shell, onyx, coral, and other materials, to form elegant designs. In prehistoric times, the Zunis made a great deal of redware pottery. Today most ceramics are coated with a white slip and decorated in complex patterns. Bowls or jars may have a break in the line surrounding the neck, since some believe that to close the line might "close" the potter's life. Stone fetishes (like little animals) are especially sought after, while there has been a minor trend towards making rustic wood furniture in recent years.

Many people come to Zuni to purchase items during the Crafts Expo, which coincides with the Intertribal Ceremonial in Gallup during August. The Zunis also hold a big fair the third weekend in August. The Shalako Ceremony in late November or early December is the most famous Zuni gathering, one of the more outstanding of all native rituals. The date is announced in October. This celebration–of–life was described in the best-selling *Dance Hall of the Dead*, and though formerly public, it may or may not be open during any given year, depending on the mood of the tribal council and governor (you had better check). The Shalako are masked dancers in bird headdresses, some 10-ft. tall, covered in robes, pinyon branches, or eagle and raven feathers. Other men smeared with grime in ragged skirts are actually comic clowns, called Mudheads. Performers may rotate in and out of houses or around blazing fires as they execute orchestrated steps, mollifying the inscrutable forces that bestow rain and fertility. Festivities last through the long night to the trance-like beat of drums (bring a warm coat). In addition, several traveling dance troupes (Nawetsa, Rainbow, etc.) operate from Zuni Pueblo, parents passing on key skills to the younger generation. Keep a lookout for periodic announcements.

A trip to Zuni is enjoyable because one can wander around the community, view the church exterior, take in galleries or museums, and drive to several lakes. Many of the craft shops, gas stations, and a café are located right on NM 53 as it goes east to west through the pueblo. Turquoise Village Store, for one, has been open since 1978. The Shiwi Trading Post is another established outlet. You'll see the Visitor Information Center and the A: shiwi A: wan Museum (782-4403; open 9 am-5:30 pm, Monday through Friday plus Saturdays in summer) on the south side of this thoroughfare, at 1222 Hwy. 53.

Evangelization at Zuni began early, during the 1620s. Turn south onto Sandy Hill St. and then Mission Ave. to find the church. Our Lady of Guadalupe (ca. 1629-1660) was rebuilt several times, the only one of three mission churches to survive here. One major reconstruction took place in the late 1960s. This locale has been visited by a long list of luminaries including Jackie Onassis. If you can get inside, leave a donation at the door, and peruse the huge murals of masked Zuni religious figures or kachinas. Backgrounds represent summer and winter. On the north wall, the sixth figure carrying the smoldering stick is the fire kachina; four warrior kachinas and two bodyguards parade behind him. Ken Seotewa is adding to and restoring these paintings. This particular building, closed on and off for yet more renovation, serviced the village of Halona. Halona is the site of the contemporary town, where the Zuni people had coalesced by 1692. After the Indian revolt of 1680, the mission was refounded in 1706. During 1754, one report states that the priest was living reasonably well from locally produced corn and mutton. Yet life slowed with different epidemics, the village almost wiped out a couple of times not only during the colonial era, but as recently as 1900. Modern interest in the area soon picked up, though, resulting in a series of excavations. A few of today's residences may be of colonial origin. They stand atop foundations hundreds of years older. To the casual observer, the overall impression resembles a crazy quilt of adobe, cinder block, or earthen textures, perhaps untidy and foreign to the western eye.

There are six reservoirs on the reservation, one or two of which make for pleasant outings. For example, turn south on Pia Mesa Road from Hwy. 53, and then west onto Ojo Caliente Road. This stretch becomes Zuni Road 2. Ojo Caliente Lake appears after the abandoned village of the same name in fourteen miles (ten are paved), an agreeable birding and fishing spot with picnic tables. Geese and ducks stop here during the transition seasons. The Hawikuh ruins are not quite visible, but they lay on the west side of the road. Or, head east on NM 53 for 11 miles, and watch for the Nutria Lakes sign onto Zuni Road 5. Trek north for seven miles. You'll have to hang a left onto a gravel track for a mile or two, climbing the access loop up a steep grade. Camping, fishing, picnicking, and limited boating are permitted at this attractive if small lake (fee $5), surrounding by scrub oak and pinyon. Actually, a second Nurtia Lake pops up further down the Rio Nutria, the unpaved access ultimately intersecting NM 602. Call the Zuni Game Department for details concerning fishing permits (782-5851). You can also keep going north on Zuni Road 5 until you arrive at the village of Lower Nutria in almost five more miles (after the lake turnoff). Upper Nutria is next in another three miles, the location of petroglyphs on the nearby cliff face, plus the scant archeological remains of a Chaco outlier called Great Kiva Village. Remnants of a couple of pueblos may be visited but you'll need permission. Black Rock Lake comes up 4 miles east of Zuni on the north side of Route 53, with a vintage dam that can be reached via NM 4.

Also south of Gallup, the Ramah Navajo Reservation dangles below NM 53 (and the main part of the vast Navajo reserve), along the eastern border of "Zuni land." The actual town of Ramah lies on the highway in a little valley. The reservation was organized in the 1860s, when the Navajos remigrated to the western part of the state after their detention at Bosque Redondo. Several thousand Navajos live here now. Mormon missionaries inaugurated the town in 1876. One bizarre tale insists that Billy the Kid wasn't shot by Pat Garrett at all, but counted out his remaining years secretively in romantic Ramah! This small community does have a handful of intriguing buildings and lovely, tall cottonwood trees. A couple of cafes open Monday through Saturday. The Ramah Museum (open 1-4 on Fridays and 10-2 on Saturdays; 783-4150), in the venerable Bond House, reposes at the corner of Bloomfield and Lewis (from the highway, cut northwest towards town for one block at the four-way intersection). You'll find displays on the background of this region set up by the local historical society. By the way, the Ramah Community Fair (775-3256; 775-3395) cranks up in late August with a parade and powwow, complimented by Navajo dancing.

Nearby points of interest include the Candy Kitchen Wolf Rescue Ranch (775-3304), twenty miles southeast of Ramah, which schedules free tours of happy rescued critters Thursday through Sunday (tours at 11 am, 1 pm, and 3 pm). This unique facility has been in operation for 10 years. Have you ever peered into the eyes of an Arctic wolf? Motor 9 miles east of Ramah on NM 53, and then south on partly paved BIA Road 125 for eight miles. Bear right (west) for four more miles on gravelly BIA Road 120.

Another BIA road, 132, heads north of Ramah for 2 miles via Bloomfield Ave. to reach Ramah Lake. Go past the museum and bend right at the tiny sign by a stone house with a porch. Be advised that the gravel track is pitted.

An access to the right hooks up with a walk to the top of the spillway. This appealing reservoir is about 15 surface acres in size, nestled among Ponderosa pine, pinyon, tamarisk, and hulking coral pink blocks of sandstone. Used originally by the Mormon settlers for irrigation, the lake has been open as a public picnicking ground since the 1980s. There's a boat ramp, but not much else in the way of facilities. You can't camp here, although Ramah Lake is stocked with bass, trout, and bluegill. Navajo families come out to fish on Sundays. A sign near the entrance advertises an adjacent campground (try the Lewis Trading Center for info, 783-4368).

To the east of Gallup, Red Rock State Park (elevation 6600 ft.; 863-1337; open daily 8 am-7 pm in summer; 8 am-4:30 pm rest of year) is a pirouette of fiery red shapes only 8 miles away. Petroglyphs and archeological sites have been discovered here. This 600-acre facility, established in the 1970s, can be a good place to sample a bit of the plateau country with its spires, escarpments, and ledges. Camping is permitted (fee: $10-14; showers and toilets), and the park even encompasses a couple of nature trails. The campground, post office, and trading post are located on the right, as one drives into the park grounds. The camping area spreads comfortably among some trees next to a dramatically sweeping rock face. A nifty hike of 2.5 miles starts immediately to the north, behind the post office. This trail involves several branches, so it may be wise to acquire the map in one of the park brochures. The historical, stone-veneered Outlaw Trading Post (863-1336), in business since 1888, stays open all day for snacks and souvenirs. The striking, skyward knobs of Church Rock hover above the hiking loop.

The park is handy to a medley of sights and events. The Gallup Intertribal Indian Ceremonial is held at this location in August using the 7500-seat rodeo arena for dancing. The facility also witnesses a powwow in May, a bull-riding contest in July, and a balloon fiesta in very late November. The Red Rock Museum and Visitor Center highlight native arts and crafts, including kachinas, rugs, ceramics, and even masks. Note that there are a few formations that are simple to spot. Kit Carson cave, a gaping hole in the middle of a cliff of Jurassic sandstone, is interesting, but it's momentarily closed to the public. Pyramid Rock bulks up to the west of the park, on the north side of the interstate. You should be able to pick out its towering mass from the frontage road. One can explore the surrounding area as well. NM

566 runs north before it swerves eastward becoming Navajo Rte. 11, connecting several administrative units called chapter houses. Problems with uranium-contaminated water have stirred the cauldron of controversy in recent times. Indian families keep sheep penned in corrals along this quiet stretch, which crosses the Continental Divide just before reaching Smith Lake. Smith Lake is the site of the Junior Rodeo on July 4, and there's a small trading post (Ashkii-tosh). The far-flung Borrego Pass Trading Post (open weekdays and Saturday mornings) beckons to the north, up NM 371 for a couple of miles and then east on part-asphalt/part-gravel Navajo Rte. 48 for roughly eight miles. If you need some beadwork, or a stovepipe for country living, drop in; look for the sign. NM 371 also points south to I-40 and a secondary highway that extends as far east as Grants. Mt. Powell (8745 ft.) will be off to your right side as you truck south into Thoreau, a ranching community that endures along old Route 66.

It's possible to wind into the Zuni Mountains from Gallup. Go twelve miles east of Gallup, veering south onto NM 400 (exit 33). A mini-plaza appears on route, housing a restaurant, gas station, pawnshop, and post office. You'll pass Fort Wingate after 3.5 miles from the interstate; turn at the Fort Wingate historical marker next to the veteran's pocket park. Several noteworthy stone buildings still stand. Fort Wingate (1860-1919), originally in San Rafael, was relocated to this spot in 1868, as Kit Carson and the army moved to expatriate the Navajo. The Navajo had exchanged assaults with both the Hispanos and incoming gringos for some time. A few Navajos avoided surrender here by squirreling away into the Four Corners. Once known as Bear Springs, the locale was eventually renamed for Capt. Benjamin Wingate, who died from wounds received in a battle with Confederate forces at Val Verde. In 1914, thousands of refugees camped on the grounds during the Mexican Revolution. General Pershing was stationed in this place for a short period. The fort enclosure was transferred to the Department of the Interior as of the 1920s, the complex being transformed into a school. The parade ground became a playground, even as the barracks were converted into dormitories.

Back on NM 400, the road gradually ascends into some scenic backcountry. Quaking Aspen campground materializes in about five miles. After two more miles (10.5 miles from the interstate), watch for the gravelly turnoff to the right or south to McGaffey Campground. These facilities remain open from late spring until the second week in September with a fourteen-day limit. The main McGaffey Campground (tables, grills, pit toilets), ensconced among Ponderosa pines, borders a pretty meadow. You can walk from the campground to the McGaffey Lookout by taking a brief hike. The Strawberry Trail (1.25-miles one way) exits from the southeast corner of the camping area, marked by an explanatory plaque. It wends over a small bridge, and then proceeds next to a log fence through Strawberry Canyon, up to the lookout tower (elevation 8137 ft.). The weekend traveler may become windblown if you climb the stairs, but you'll attain a fine view of some dense woodland. These mountains are an ancient uplift with a Precambrian core of granite. Overlaying sediments were chiseled into sandstone clefts, and later on, big lava flows sputtered to a halt over huge sections of the surrounding region.

On the other hand, you can stick with NM 400 as it becomes well-graveled C.R. 50. McGaffey Lake (7600 ft.; 287-8833) lies only a half mile or so past the campground turnoff. This pond of 13-surface acres and a pier has attracted trout fans and picnickers for over fifty years. One or two little trails trickle out from the reservoir, while a couple of old summer homes cling to the side of the roadway. If you plug away on C.R. 50, the sign for the McGaffey Lookout Tower comes up in another mile. This particular lookout is one of the most reachable towers in the entire state. A dirt track heads to the right approaching the structure after a mile, and for some piney air, stroll this access route through the silent forest.

Quemado

Population: 700
Elevation: 7000 ft.
Distance from Albuquerque: 148 miles
Quemado Ranger District: 773-4678

The shortest drive to Quemado traces I-40 west to Hwy. 117, and then south through the black and blistered lava flow of the El Malpais National Monument. You will pass the pastel-colored natural arch of La Ventana on the way, where it's possible to make a rest stop. Eventually one ploughs through a remote stretch called the North Plains. Cows idle amidst blades of wavering muhly, grama, and barley grasses, as ranch horses canter between clumps of tan and silvery-green brushy ground-cover. Crows squawk overhead. The famous Lightning Field is not visible from the road, but it's nearby, a piece of environmental art from the 1970s consisting of 400 shiny steel poles placed into the earth to attract lightning (call 773-4560 or 898-3335 to make reservations for a home-steader's cabin; lightning displays occur in summer). East of Quemado is the general region of the ancient Datil-Mogollon volcanic field. Large rocky cliffs hem this lonesome portion of Hwy. 60, composed of volcanic ash that has occasionally eroded into weird pinnacles scalloped by juniper. Younger, slightly less chiseled volcanic landscapes fill the area to the west of Quemado. Plump patches of handsome forest grow some distance to the south.

General

The village of Quemado—which means burnt—may have been the namesake of a local creek that was in turn called Rito Quemado because of a brush fire that blackened both its banks. José Padilla's sheep ranch appears to have been the nucleus of the original Hispanic settlement; several aspiring *rancheros* followed Padilla's lead. Rito Quemado, from the late nineteenth century, took advantage of an established cattle-herding track to Magdalena. The title was alternately shortened to Rito by the late 1800s, and then to Quemado after 1901. Other stories suggest that the name came from a smoldering coal deposit, or even an Apache chief with a blistered hand. Whatever the explanation, Quemado is not the place to go if you want to rock and roll in luxury or cultural activity.

When satellites glaze over the earth taking photographs, the heavily populated east and west coasts of the United States are ablaze with light. But western New Mexico is an ocean of darkness at night. It's perhaps the inkiest spot in the nation, because Catron County, while New Mexico's biggest county and larger than the state of Hawaii, has very few folks in it (around 3500). So why come to Quemado? For one thing, this is a scenically varied part of the state. Mountain woods, high desert canyons, and grassy tablelands are all close to each other, great for an out-of-the-way couple of days. And the darkness is good for stargazing. In summer, the Milky Way forms a bright gooey gash from the northeast to the southwest sky, discernible because the plane of our solar system tilts at an angle, relative to the plane of the galaxy as a whole. And relaxing, since the nearby sierras and lakes do not jam up with people as much as the Sandias except for July (especially Independence Day). Winters can be somewhat cold. Quemado Lake campgrounds are generally closed at that time. Some say that the goldfish from a new pond have escaped into the lake, adversely affecting catches. Others insist that the fish are biting by early spring. Summer weekends witness more activity than weekdays.

Fall is the time for excellent big game hunting, and outfitters do a pretty good business, clients coming from many states. Controversy surrounds the importation of animals from elsewhere, since a group of elk from Colorado had to be quarantined. Bear, deer, antelope, and elk all inhabit the mountains or trickle into the steppe. The elk grow enormous racks that are sought after by hunters, the bigger the better (if you decide to charge around preferred hunting areas in October, wear an orange hat). Each year these antlers sprout anew, sometimes developing at the extraordinary rate of an inch per day. Don't miss the curious stack of antlers on the north side of the main drag next to the Chevron.

Quemado has marginal amenities, but one can buy gas here or pick up bait, tackle, and sporting goods. There's a small grocery decorated by more antlers, and a couple of country stores hawk collectibles or second hand stuff. One or two interesting adobes look abandoned. Several sturdy structures are built of stone.

Practicalities

El Serape (open until 9 pm but closed Saturdays after 4 pm and Sundays; 773-4620) is the principal eatery on the north side of the highway, where you can chow down on New Mexican entrees beneath an intact pressed tin ceiling. Mexican blankets and old photos adorn the walls. The Largo Café (open 7 am to 9 pm everyday; 773-4686), on the south side of US 60 next to the motel of the same name, cooks up standards. Snuffy's Restaurant (773-4672) is 17 miles south of town, down 32 and east on 103, on the way to Quemado Lake. This place advertises itself as a steak-house and serves potables, burgers, and snacks for lunch and dinner during the tourist months (March through November, more or less). Snuffy's also operates a gas station and convenience store with hunting and fishing licenses, bait, etc. Cottontails hop around the parking lot. Snuffy even handles a limited boat rental service and a few RV slots. It would be extremely prudent to bring some food from Albuquerque if you plan on spending any time here.

Quemado has three basic motels. The Allegre (north side of Hwy. 60) is distinguished by a teeny rock garden protected by a wooden flamingo. Allison's Motel (773-4550), on the south side, proffers candy and morning coffee, while the Largo Motel sits off to the western edge of town. The Sunset RV Park is close by. Rooms at these establishments run in the $30-40 range. Small pets seem to be ok but should be declared at the desk.

Things to do

The Lightning Field management rents an office in Quemado in a white, two-story building next to El Serape, and the folks who run this facility make a pick-up during their busy season at about 2:30-3:00 pm in the afternoon. Walter de María designed the project. Scientists believe that no two lightning bolts ever array in quite the same manner, often putting out "jets" or discharges of varying colors at temperatures hotter than the sun. This macabre dance of nature represents an ever-changing pattern of arching splendor and power that bewitches photographers. Sporadic exhibits describe how the Lightning Field was constructed and may contain dramatic (and of course striking) pictures or postcards.

Quemado Lake State Park lies south of town (elevation 7800 ft.; 773-4678). The reservoir is small (130 acres), but it's scenic, situated high up enough to be surrounded by woodland. The lake, created by damming Largo Creak during the 1970s, is located in the east-west range called the Gallo Mountains, named for the wild turkeys that proliferate here, periodically delighting hikers. The Gallos make up a northern portion of the Mogollon Plateau, an uplifted wedge that penetrates far into Arizona. Go south on Hwy. 32 for 14.2 miles, to the Quemado Lake sign. Then head east (left) for 4 paved miles. You will run into the main parking lot, with its adjacent ramp for electric motor boats. Rainbow trout fishing is the chief activity along with camping, picnicking, and hiking. If you continue around the lake to the left or east side you'll find a series of campgrounds (RV and tent) along the well-graveled forest road. Cove Campground is first.

Juniper Campground ($10-15 fee; grills; toilets) is second on the northeast side of the lake, and has two paths leading down to the water. Piñon Campground appears next. Stay on the forest road and bear left, or southeast, to reach the three-part El Caso Campground (no fee; fire rings) and picnic area, which spills along El Caso Creek. El Caso remains open through mid-fall, whereas the other venues close earlier. Autumn is gorgeous, with temperate days. Note that the range between daytime high and evening low is wider than in Albuquerque, and night temperatures can dip way below freezing in October. The Largo Trail (about 3 miles long) commences at El Caso Campground #1, encircling the lake's farthest shore and trucking up to the fire tower. Dense stands of Ponderosa pine, cottonwood, pinyon, and oak enfold the campsites. Purple summer wildflowers dapple the forested byway that extends to form an unpaved network, which swings around to either Escondido Mountain to the north (via F.R. 13D, a.k.a. Baca Rd.), or the Mangas Mountains and Slaughter Mesa to the south (via F.R. 13). Forest Road 13 ties into both F.R. 854 and F.R. 93. These routes may be pursued to the west to reconnect with the highway. From the El Caso Camp-

Quemado Lake

ground, one can simply stroll along F.R. 13 for quite a distance as it unwinds to more primitive camping spots.

Or, return to the park entrance, and check out the undeveloped shores of the lake. It's feasible to follow a fishing trail hugging the water's edge that starts from the prime parking area. Look for the restroom, where you'll see a path up to the spillway, leading to a little sign at the far end. An amble down the shoreline takes several minutes. Ospreys fly overhead now and then. Eventually one hits an option to continue right, away from the reservoir onto the Lake Overlook Trail. You will pass through a barbed wire fence access as you penetrate the woods, with a chance to sit down at a bench overlook approximately 40 minutes from the point of origin at the spillway. A secondary trail pops up to the right a few minutes later, which heads west to the El Caso Tower Lookout (at this writing, this turnoff is not marked by a sign). If you stay on the main trail, one climbs over a culvert. You veer to the left up the side of a rise, obtaining some fine views of the surrounding piney mesas. There's a nice vista of the lake at the end roughly 30-40 minutes from tower turnoff (adding up to maybe 2.5 miles from the spillway to the finish). The reverse trip takes less time and effort because you'll be going downhill as you backtrack. The Quemado Ranger office graciously gave me a sketch map of the trail system free of charge, but my experience of these hikes does not quite jibe with their diagram or directional orientation. Trails here are being improved and lengthened, which could account for the discrepancy.

Hwy. 32 keeps going south through Jewett Gap, a high point on the way to the microdot of Apache Creek, dubbed for the stream that created this narrow valley. The Apaches dominated the vicinity for a long time. A network of regional forts was set up to control them once and for all, as Americans rolled in to exploit promising mines. One encounters some real woodland in lieu of mesas for a while. Eleven miles south of the Quemado Lake turnoff, F.R. 770 jogs to the right (west) for several miles to the lookout atop Fox Mountain (9200 ft.) . There's some primitive camping along this fairly well graded but sandy track into Lawson Canyon. The area is part of the lovely Apache National Forest, actually administered through the Gila National Forest office at Silver City (388-8201). Forest Road 93 crops up a mile later, and it snakes a long way to the east past Gallo Peak up to Slaughter Mesa. Locals maintain that the elk are especially active along this stretch either very early in the morning or in the evening, as they come down from the mesa to forage.

Another gravelly forest road bobs up in two miles that wanders over some grassland into Hardcastle Gap, a break in the mountains. NM 32 echoes the creekbed. Picturesque log houses evoke the erstwhile Saturday afternoon world of B-movie westerns. Hunting outfitters, organic farms, youth camps, and ranches with shallow pastures, all fringe the highway, which swerves through a section of beautiful cliffs. In autumn, the oak, narrowleaf cottonwood, and locust trees burst with a tawny, burnished gold, the color of fine sherry. The oak trees produce an acorn that was once ground by the Indians and the pioneers. When the oak flour was combined with cornmeal and water, the batter made tolerable pancakes or porridge. You'll find a gas station at the country store in Apache Creek. Signs point to nearby camping alternatives. Here one picks up NM 12 as it turns to the southwest roughly paralleling the often-dry Tularosa River, speckled by a few old adobe homes and alligator juniper.

The forests in this part of the state can seem completely removed from, and unaffected by, civilization. Nonetheless, prehistoric communities thrived 1600 to a thousand years ago in western Catron County. The umbrella term Mogollon culture covers prehistoric development in southern New Mexico. This region was for a time the most densely occupied portion of the state. The famed villages of the Mimbres valley a tad to the east evolved a little later. People in the Reserve area lived in spacious pithouses, rooms shoveled out of the earth roofed with timber and brush, and they fashioned enormous quantities of red pottery. One site in particular excavated during the 1930s left behind exceptionally large numbers of heavy stone mortars for grinding corn (infinitesimal particles of stone mixed in with the corn usually ground away at tooth surfaces also). Eventually these folks expanded in number. They filled up drainages and concentrated more into aboveground, contiguous-room pueblos, making lots of black-on-white ceramics. Actually, at least three types of pottery styles have been labeled for the town of Reserve.

Today's Reserve (elevation 5770 ft.), established once again in the 1870s as Upper San Francisco Plaza, now has gas stations, an emporium, a bar, churches, cute restaurants, motels, and the rather dreary Catron County Courthouse. A couple of Victorian adobes lend real charm to this remote locale. Look for the county fair here with its championship goats the third week in August. Carmen's is a popular café open every day, replete with hunting photos and homey bric-a-brac next to a gift shop. Reserve originally encompassed two other related hamlets, namely San Francisco Plaza and Lower San Francisco Plaza, both further south on NM 435 (which becomes F.R. 141 as it ascends into the Kelly and Mogollon Mountains). These two interconnected villages date to the 1850s. You'll discover an historical cemetery at the St. Francis Pastoral Center as well as a small RV park. Satellite dishes now arise next to the horse barns and vintage adobes of pretty Negrito Creek. Outlaws of the nineteenth century including Butch Cassidy used hideouts to the south along NM 12 and US 180.

To the west of Quemado, there are spots that may appeal to outdoor buffs. For example, one can visit Zuni Salt Lake. Drive about a mile west of Quemado as measured from the Hwy. 32 intersection. Leaving Hwy. 60, turn north onto a paved route marked 601. At 1.5 miles past the turnoff, the road becomes gravel, but it's level and wide, and should be ok for passenger cars if the weather has been clear and dry. At the 6.5 point you clip the northeast corner of the Eagle Peak Wilderness Area, a big chunk of terrain currently being studied by the Bureau of Land Management. The casual visitor will want to stay on the primary road. You might see cows, rabbits, or antelopes, not to mention the occasional photogenic windmill. Just before mile marker 18 there is a branch. Take the left fork onto a washboardy side-track, and ignore the crisscrossing maze of less well-defined choices. The weekend traveler will then spy the lake on your left side after .75 mile or so. You can park on the short approach turnout to the left. This tiny lake was formed in a collapsed volcanic caldera (the magma hitting a pocket of under-ground water causing an explosion), and because the water had no outlet, the salt content achieved considerable density. Prehistoric Indians collected highly-prized salt here, as did Spanish explorers in 1540.

A few archeological sites (consisting mostly of scattered artifacts like worked rocks) date as far back as 6,000 BC, when bands of hardy hunter-gatherers trekked the far reaches of New Mexico. These migrating groups sorely depended on certain types of stone that could be knapped into spear points and even knives. The remains of scant shelters have been discovered within the broader region also. Meanwhile cinder cones and basalt forma-tions attest to the vulcanism that characterizes so much of the western part of the state. These shapes protrude among sandstone mesas and rolling grass-lands. The lake is integrated into the belief system of the Zuni people, who claim the area, though it falls south of the formal reservation boundary. A quick jaunt around the lake almost makes for an informal hike. The Zuni are now trying to protect the locality from aggressive coal mining interests.

Moving east of Quemado, the weekend traveler will cruise into Pie Town (elevation 8,000 ft.) in 21 miles on Hwy 60. The Pie-O-Neer Café (open 7-7; closed Friday; 772-2900) offers over a dozen kinds of pie from cherry to peanut butter cream, plus breakfast, a few groceries, and knickknacks. For those who seek amusement in terms of a flaky crust, this place should be on your list. The name Pie Town was kickstarted back in the 1920s when a gold miner (some think a gas station proprietor) began baking pies to shore up his diminishing income. About 70 people live in the vicinity. The restau-rant really took off when an Albuquerque resident moved here during the early 1990s, armed with a book of her grandma's recipes. Pie Town even has

Stopping for a pie in Pie Town

—you guessed it—a Pie Festival the second Saturday of September, pulling in 800-1000 folks for barbeques and horned toad races. In addition, New Mexico astronomers have constructed a radio telescope antenna in Pie Town to study the emissions from distant stars. This effort expands the famous VLA system closer to Socorro that will eventually string, in one form or another, across the entire state. There's a campground (Jackson Park) situated on the south side of the highway.

Beyond Pie Town, after one crosses the Continental Divide, the Sawtooth Mountains emerge first, a branch of the Datil Mountains, which erupt a little further to the east. Box canyons of high desert are edged with knife-like spires, part of a large informal wilderness relished by savvy southwest enthusiasts. The two mountain groups consist of conglomerate and sandstone, low peaks that top out at around seven to nine thousand ft.. These cordilleras provide some confection for the eye and a boundary for the gigantic basin that unfolds further along Hwy. 60. Forest Road 6A appears 12 miles before

Datil (30 miles east of Quemado). This well-graded byway affords an eyeful of serrated Sawtooth Peak at four miles in. You'll run into a dry wash after another two miles if you keep going. You can roam the wash for a casual hike in favorable weather. Stream edges may display the tracks of animals searching for water. Bears, skunks, and raccoons make plantigrade, or flat, tracks with five distinct toes in a single curving line. Bobcats prowl more on their tiptoes, and leave round prints with four toe pads (in two "rows" rather than one) and a rear main pad. Coyote tracks also show four toe pads and a rear pad, but are more level than the bobcat's, and smaller, like a dog's. Deer or elk create hoofed tracks that resemble slots. If you're interested, primitive camping occurs at turnouts close to the highway wedged among pinyon trees. Another gravel road, F.R. 6, is located three miles further east (nine miles west of Datil), indicated by a small sign. This route reaches north into some semi-high country, following the base of the mountain. One fork veers west (left) into Hay Canyon after about 1 and .5 miles. If you continue straight for another mile, the weekend traveler should pass a batch of trailers before bumping into the sign for the fire lookout. The steep 2-mile drive to Davenport Peak (9,355 ft.) ought to be handled only in a vehicle with good traction, although if you have time, walking these switchbacks should satisfy your exercise requirements. The staff at the Magdalena Ranger Station (854-2281) or the Quemado Ranger Station can sell you maps of these areas that depict the numerous sidetracks.

Datil was the home of a fort in 1888 that was built to protect settlers from Apache raids. A mile west of Datil, or twenty miles east of Pie Town, the Datil Wells Recreation Site materializes on the south side of the highway. This pleasant public use area is 640 acres in size, and the Bureau of Land Management in Socorro maintains a ten-acre campground (835-0412; water; tables; fire rings; $5 fee) at the site of one of the wells, dug to refresh sheep and cattle. There were fifteen such wells at one time. The historical livestock trail once hooked into an important railhead at Magdalena, where the cattle could be shipped out to various markets. A three-mile nature hike exits from the rear of the campground, with an opportunity to return at the half-way point. It twines among pinyon and juniper woodlands to expose three overlooks of the vast, buff-colored San Agustín Plain.

Carrizozo / Capitan

Population of Carrizozo: 1,200
Elevation: 5426 ft.
Distance from Albuquerque: 149 miles
Carrizozo Travel Center (Chamber of Commerce): 648-2732

Depending on which way you come, multi-colored rocks and soils define a high desert terrain spotted with both occasional sinkholes (actually the collapsed ceilings of underground caverns) and outcrops of rugged granite. Carrizozo itself sits at a sort of interface. Just to the west lies one of the dramatic volcanic landscapes that bristle up intermittently within the "basin and range" part of the state. To the east, the relatively level steppe of the Great Plains gradually phases into view. If you make an approach from the western portion of US 380, the dark lava flow surges before you, a black sea lapping at the base of the mountains. The Sacramento Range is considered to be the major cordillera hereabouts (some ninety miles long), and the Jicarillas to the northeast are often classified as one of their sub-ranges. Looming up from the south, magnificent Sierra Blanca (12,003 ft.) is a huge, isolated volcanic mass within the Sacramentos. It projects 8,000 ft. above the long Tularosa Valley, which unfurls like an attenuated limb prickled by Alamogordo on the way to El Paso.

General

Carrizozo is one of those places you can probably do during the cooler portion of the year. That is, unless you want to spend time in the mountains. According to accepted theory, *carizo* was the Spanish word applied to the area's reed grass. Cattle ranches sprouted in the vicinity to take advantage of this resource during the 1870s-90s. Then the El Paso and Northeastern Railroad extended its line here in 1899, thus inaugurating the town by generating jobs and a modest boom. The name was coined when a cowhand added the last syllable-"zo"- to carizo to denote the abundant rangeland (mimicking Spanish syntax), at the same time the community was actually platted (1906). The busy years ebbed with a railroad strike during the 1920s. The conversion from steam to diesel engines wiped out more jobs by the 1950s. Carrizozo held on through the coming decades as a shipping and commercial center, attempting to develop its tourist trade with some piecemeal improvements.

Today, two highways popular with truckers intersect at the northern terminus of this small crossroads locale. Several motels, three gas stations, and no less than three (count 'em) convenience stores abide at the junction. As the county seat, Carrizozo could use a few extra trees and polish (a little public art?) to beguile more weekend visitors through this natural gateway of the state's southern deserts and cordilleras. A trend towards renovating its older buildings represents a step in the right direction. In the meantime a few artists have moved into vintage buildings on the east side of town near the railroad. A plethora of wildlife, such as the oryx (imported from Africa), pronghorn antelope, mule deer, and barbary sheep inhabit the region, attracting hunters. These animals are sometimes visible from the road if one ventures off of the principal routes. Be careful of these unpaved stretches in places like White Oaks after a snow. Stay on the main street, and let the little sidetracks dry out for a while, or you could get stuck in the mud. On the other hand, if you come during the summer, Miner's Day is celebrated at White Oaks the first Saturday in June.

Practicalities

The Four Winds Restaurant (6 am-9 pm everyday; 648-2964) at the junction of US 380 and US 54 griddles up roadhouse standards and southwest entrees. Joe's (east side of US 54) does expresso and sandwiches, while Paul's Coffee Cup cooks New Mexican fare at the south end of town. Roy's Ice Cream Parlor (8:30 am-6 pm Mon-Fri; 10:30 am-4:30 pm Sat) lives on at 1200 Ave. E, featuring its original 1935 Liquid Carbonic Fountain. Roy reveres the chocolate malt with toppings, syrups, and alchemical confections secreted into gleaming silver compartments. The Outpost Bar and Grill (415 Central, or the east side of US 54) is a real standby here. If you ever wanted to dine among a bunch of critter heads like a Wild West saloon, this place should be experienced within your present incarnation, as the busts of buffalo and caribou are interspersed between bugles and guns. Menu selections are confined mostly to hamburgers, steaks, and chicken strip sandwiches. There's also a taco stand in the Texaco Mini-mart on the south side of US 380.

The Four Winds Motel (648-2356) claims the northwestern side of the chief intersection and offers decent if basic rooms with cable television. The Crossroads Motel operates across the street, whereas the relatively quiet Sands Motel-RV Park (648-4000) lies about a quarter mile south of town on US 54. Rates at these establishments run in the $30-40 range. The newer and fairly busy Rainbow Inn (648-4006; $40-60 range) is tucked behind the Four Winds Restaurant at the southeast corner of the main junction. It provides nicely-sized units with the homey touch of a microwave and mini-frig in addition to cable TV.

Things to do

Historical buildings from the early 1900s symbolize Carrizozo's optimism from an earlier day, should you wish to walk or drive around for a few minutes. Central Ave. (US 54 in town) hits E Ave. at the 1100 block. Hang a right (west) on E Ave. where US 54 bends sharply to the left. In the middle of this block is the Long Tin Shop, a picturesque frame building from 1906. Follow E Ave. to the corner of 11th St. to find the Masonic Building (1907). This structure was put up by William McDonald, New Mexico's first elected state governor. As of 1846, New Mexico became a territory of the United States; it was formally, finally, and somewhat uneasily admitted to the union in 1912. Just west stands the pink Tiffany-Thornton house (1000 E Ave.), dating to 1905. Across the street (411 10th St.) you'll see the Petty-Ziegler home, a Mediterranean style place of adobe bricks. Six blocks further west on E and to the left, one can check out the Spence House (ca.1909) at 701 Drexel. This unevenly revivified manse was the residence of well-to-do sheep rancher Clarence Spence, and a teeny dragon tops the light standard. Return down E and take a left (north) at 10th for two blocks. The grid from 10th St. to 13th St. retains a sprinkling of cottages, mostly adobe but with the characteristic touches (such as wood stripping) of prolific local builder Frank English. Go right at 3rd Ave., and then right again on 11th for a couple of blocks. Frank English's home (ca. 1912) still exists at 404 11th St. behind the metal fence. English designed the Spense House. Frank Lutz, a sheep rancher, constructed the Lutz Bldg. at 401 12th St. (east of Central or US 54) for $35,000. Frank English managed this place as a store and upstairs dance hall when the unfortunate Lutz went broke. The rectangle of partly bordered-up streets skirting the railroad is undergoing a bit of rehabilitation as studio space. A red brick edifice to the north, on the heels of the Rainbow Inn, is slated to become a history museum. And don't forget the Sierra Blanca Brewing Company back down the road at 503 12th St., New Mexico's largest microbrewery (there are about 20), open for tasting of its nut-brown beer and root beer Monday-Friday. The building, once used as a hotel, theatre, and garage, harkens to 1917. Peak to the rear of the Outpost Café or call 648-6606 for details.

East of town, the gorgeous White Mountain Wilderness of 48,000 acres envelops the north end of the Sacramento Mountains, which spike up from the desert floor. This lush spine was glaciated during Pleistocene times. The plant life includes mountain mahogany at the lower elevations, and Ponderosa pine followed by the aspen and spruce higher up, as in much of the southwest. Box elders and willows grow along the watercourses. Unlike many ranges, though, this one sneaks in a pleasant pause next to a body of water, namely Bonito Lake, a secluded sanctum that drowned the ghost town of Bonito City. The reservoir, now owned by the city of Alamogordo, was created by the railroad in 1929. To get there, drive 8 miles east on 380, then 13 miles south on NM 37. You'll observe an RV campground and the sign for the Monjeau Shadows B and B on the way. Just before the village of Angus, head right (west) onto F.R. 107 (also known as C.R. 9, the main point of entry to the wilderness from the east side). Proceed for 3 miles to the lake on a recently repaved surface. The Mills Canyon Trail comes up in about a mile or so, exiting from a picnicking-parking area. Monjeau Peak Lookout can be reached in 5 miles from this trailhead. Bonito Lou's Café, a little further in, turns on the oven during the summer. You can wind around the lake to encounter a primitive campground that's open well into the fall ($10). After 1.8 paved miles the weekend traveler will bump into a fork. Two more camping opportunities ($7-12) are available during the warm months only, namely Westlake and then Southfork, located a very short

Sierra Blanca Peak between Capitan and Carrizozo

distance to the left. The Argentina–Bonito Trailhead is positioned 3.3 more miles to the right along Bonito Creek. These lovely canyons become the temporary preserve of bald eagles that fly down from the northern Rockies during the chilly portion of the year. For more info, contact the Lincoln National Forest Smokey Bear Station (257-4095).

In five more miles on NM 37, another alternative heads right (west) onto NM 532 reaching the Sierra Blanca Ski Resort. Sierra Blanca, once the extreme edge of the ice pack a dozen millennia ago, is the most southerly mountain of this altitude (twelve thousand ft.) in the United States. The drive to the top makes for a spectacular 12-mile dalliance with hairpin turns. The glass, wood, and stone snack bar, now run by the Apaches, opens up in winter. Actually, the gondola used to carry visitors in summer, but the management wasn't making enough to justify year-round hours. Nevertheless, you'll discover camping options along this byway. An overlook with benches a quick jog before the lodge turnoff will afford the weekend traveler an unforgettable vista of the Ruidoso Valley. A hike (four miles one-way) commences immediately prior to the entrance gate snaking up to the Lookout Mountain observation area. White Sands as well as the lava flows of the Tularosa Basin sprawl below.

Three Rivers National Recreation Area (525-4300) forms a hearty contrast to the White Mountain Wilderness, a desert playground to the south kissed with yucca and noted for its petroglyphs, one of the largest groupings in the Southwest. The Indigo Lizard Gallery sells soda pop and artistic doings at the highway turnoff. The Three Rivers Ranch, once owned by the Coghlan family, encompassed this part of the Tularosa Basin, a big time cattle outfit of the late 1800s that obtained rustled steers from Billy the Kid. Range wars were pulverizing the ranks of the locals at that time, generating the grist for Hollywood scriptwriters of a later day. Go south on US 54 for 27 miles, then east on B-30 for 4 miles.

The original Coghlan mansion, bought by Albert Fall of the Teapot Dome scandal in the 1920s (illegal oil leases that made the Interior Secretary wealthy), has been torn down. The next ranch owner built the adobe house (1 mile in) during the 1940s. In 3 more miles, watch for the turn into a picnicking-RV area (restrooms), a desirable spot from autumn through spring decorously laced with desert plants. A steep trail (1/2-mile one-way) heads to the top of a rocky ridge. The climb, which starts next to the tiny info office, is embedded within 15,000 petroglyphs of lizards, deer, and ceremonial figures, reminders of the Mogollon people who once thrived across southern New Mexico. These pictographs were chiseled over 600 years ago. Hundreds of spirally images line the path. Another side trail leads to a partly excavated multi-room adobe structure some 800 years old. Santo Niño Chapel may be seen 3.5 miles further down the main access route, while a second campsite emerges in another five miles, twelve miles from US 54.

White Oaks, so dubbed for the trees that gulped sustenance from a nearby spring, is one of the better-known and most interesting ghost towns in New Mexico. White Oaks puts on a studio tour in April (648-2985). A small Miner's Museum greets you on the way into town. Head north on US 54 for 3 miles, and then northeast on NM 349 for nine miles through the mid-sized Jicarilla Mountains. You will drive past Carrizo Mountain (to the right) and the evocative Cedarvale cemetery; Governor W.C. McDonald (mentioned above) is buried here. White Oaks has a handful of existing structures along several streets that are cradled by the surrounding peaks.

Placer gold was discovered in the vicinity as early as 1850. A gold deposit found in 1869 ignited a tent community, soon replaced by more sub-

The old schoolhouse in White Oaks

stantial dwellings (about 200) as the riches poured in. White Oaks became one of the largest bergs in the state for a few effervescent moments, reaching a population of 4,000. Pat Garrett was the sheriff. The Exchange Bank Bldg., ruthlessly denuded of its stone facade, even now commands White Oak Ave. Pressed tin sheathing has been tacked onto the front. A proud brick schoolhouse confronts you two blocks to the left, and the Queen-Ann-style Gum residence, built with timber money, is visible further up the hillside. Off the southeast side of the main drag stands the very much intact, but debatably haunted, Hoyle House, a red brick fortress erected in 1887-1893 at a cost of $50,000, purportedly for the benefit of Hoyle's sweetheart (a retired schoolteacher has lived here recently). Watson Hoyle was part owner of the Old Abe Gold Mine, perhaps the deepest gold mine in the United States, which yielded $3,000,000.

Don't miss the two-room White Oaks Bar, one of the funkier little watering holes in New Mexico. A sign firmly declares "no scum allowed." Acceptable patrons imbibe beneath a punched tin ceiling and clap to live music on sporadic Saturday evenings. White Oaks began to fade after twenty years as the mines played out. A major blow came when the El Paso Line decided to lay track at Carrizozo instead of here, due to the outrageous prices the locals wanted to extract from the railroad moguls for real estate.

A rough but moderately passable road (F.R. 72) leaves from the rear of White Oaks, past a gallery, and arches to the left around Castle Garden Mesa and Ancho Peak. You then slip by the ghost village of Reventon, and at Jicarilla, look for the 1890s false-front post office at 12 miles in. These settlements were mining spinoffs, residents even now scrounging gold dust from placer deposits (alluvial/glacial pockets with mineral particles obtainable by washing or panning). One winds up at Ancho in 19 miles; Ancho can also be approached 21 miles to the north of Carrizozo via Hwy. 54. Ancho was conceived to service the railroad, but really sprang to life with the exposure of a fire clay deposit that inspired a major brick plant. A 1930s school constructed from local brick resists the passage of time at one end of town. The train depot has been turned into an informal community museum, My House of Old Things, open during the warmer half of the year.

The Valley of Fires State Park (fee; 648-2241) is situated four miles to the west of Carrizozo on Hwy. 380. Best handled during the temperate seasons, this exotic mating of desert biology and windswept basalt embodies some of the most recent volcanic activity in the United States outside of Hawaii. In fact, Valley of Fires vies for this distinction with the El Malpais Monument. Little Black Peak, four miles to the northwest, was the small volcano (now a cinder cone) that produced the 44-mile long rumpled cloak of tar-colored rock. The park encompasses 127 square miles. The blistered surface, which exhibits many of its writhing original features, leaked into being 1,000-1,500 years ago. A few hardy plants have squeezed out an existence among tiny wedges of blown-in silt. An easy walk starts at the group shelter. Hiking the .75-mile Malpais Nature Trail (half is paved and ok for wheelchairs) helps one to appreciate the specialized adaptations that plants and animals can make to harsh conditions. A couple of the junipers are hundreds of years old, and the sotol with its lemon-colored flowers may grow to a stem height of eight feet or more here. There's also a two-mile hike on the other side of 380 that opens on an intermittent basis, a trail one-time-only visitors have probably missed. It begins a quarter mile closer to Carrizozo behind a locked gate that's momentarily without a sign. Because the state and BLM have faced delays purchasing this tract (the owner is demanding a lot), the trail lacks regular use and may be tricky to follow. An old moonshiner's cabin decays on route. Be sure to take water and a compass, or just go for a short distance and return the way you came. Back at the main carpark, there are 19 developed but shadeless campsites (mixture of tent and RV at $5 and up) supplying picnic shelters-grills-water. A nondescript visitor center with a restroom stocks plenty of books and a few gifts.

The little community of Capitan comes up twenty miles east of Carrizozo on Hwy. 380. At about 169 miles from Albuquerque, Capitan is an accessible weekend stopover that is slightly closer than the much-hyped, former hippie community of Ruidoso. Ruidoso has mushroomed in the last few years, bulging with two-dozen motels or lodges, shops, and fine restaurants. The posh La Lorraine at 2523 Sudderth Drive (the principal drag in Ruidoso) has been open since 1985, known for its pepper steak and lamb dishes. The Clare Bay Trading Co. (2710 Sudderth) competes with expensive patio dining. Ruidoso, six times the size of Capitan, occupies some stunning country. It's a reasonable destination if you want more commotion, and numerous Texans vacation in or own real estate around Ruidoso. One also has the wry convenience of fast food joints, not to mention the Billy the Kid Casino (the buffet is a good deal).

Low-key Capitan (population 800), however, is not without a whisper of humble charm. Mines proliferated a mite to the northwest as of the 1880s. Gold-bearing strata were observed at Vera Cruz Mountain, a subset of the Jicarilla Range, off the north side of US 380 some ten miles east of Carrizozo. Seaborn Gray homesteaded the Capitan area, initiating a post office in 1894. The road to Capitan skims an old railroad spur built in 1897-99 by the same line that serviced Carrizozo. Railroad promoter and local developer Charles Eddy deemed the place Capitan in 1900, borrowing the name from the nearby mountains to the east. The train hauled primarily coal until the mines died out within several years. Capitan wasn't incorporated until 1941. It now caters to ranches in the vicinity, managing a rodeo ring and a county fair held in late August. The town's chief attraction is the Smokey the Bear State Park right on Hwy. 380, open daily 9 am-5 pm, with an interpretive trail that takes one to Smokey's venerated gravesite. Smokey passed into history in 1976, but his journey to fame began in 1950 after a forest conflagration. The bear was adopted by a game warden, and then by a zoo, and he lived to become the focus of the most successful woodland conservation campaign ever launched in the United States. The Smokey Gift Shop (102 Smokey

Bear Blvd.) is only one of several stores that may be inspected, one or two of which advertise collectibles, great for piddling away an hour.

Inns here include, of course, the Smokey Bear Motel, which features some handmade furniture (316 W. Smokey Bear Blvd; $40 range; 354-2253). The Raymond Gilmer Lodge (321 W. Smokey Bear Blvd; 354-2583) is a bed and breakfast. A dozen miles to the south along Hwy. 48 in Alto, the High Country Lodge ($60-100 range; 336-4321) keeps cabins with an indoor pool, while the Sierra Mesa Lodge ($90-100 range; 336-4515) represents an exceptional bed and breakfast experience. The imaginative Sierra Mesa, loaded with Victorian and French country antiques, maintains a hot tub. Overnighters may also engage accommodation at Elk Run Cabins in Alto.

Café choices are limited. Hotel Changos (corner of Smokey Bear Blvd. and Lincoln St.) opens up on weekends for brunch, a romantic meal in a Victorian setting. This place has been written up in a couple of food columns. El Paisano (442 W. Smokey Bear Blvd.) serves Mexican entrees at the west end of town. Smokey Bear Restaurant (310 Smokey Bear Blvd.; open 7am-8 pm), festooned with pictures of guess-who, cranks out all three meals everyday. A Taco Bell Express (420 West Smokey Bear Blvd.) assists those in a hurry. Unfortunately, Spanky's (101 Smokey Bear Blvd.) seems to have closed, so you'll have to find your grilled shrimp over linguine elsewhere, but rumors are circulating that this restaurant might reopen soon. Laurie's Grill constitutes another option.

There are several outdoorsy spots in the vicinity of Capitan. To the south, go four miles to the east and then a mile south on NM 214 (a.k.a. NM 220). You should be able to see parking for the Capitan and Lincoln Trailheads on the east side. Capitan Trail, a meandering equestrian hike of 7.5 miles, could be too long for foot travelers, but you can certainly enjoy some of it, and then backtrack. Crossing the road to a gate, the path prances over beautiful grasslands. A few areas are steep and rocky. The first segment runs for 1.6 miles, bearing left along a fenceline, over a pasture and arroyo to the southwest, and then 600 feet up a ridge, gaining a view of the Bonito Valley. You then clamber down a drainage, looping under a powerline across a two-track road entering a World War II prisoner of war camp. Note the huge swimming pool!? You parallel Fort Stanton for some minutes. One then heads north following a broad canyon for two miles, eventually descending once again for something like four miles back around to the parking area. The BLM office in Roswell (627-0272) will send the weekend traveler a brochure on this hike free of charge. A glassed-in map at the carpark gives you a pretty fair idea of this route plus several other trails. Although the trail is marked in a few places by fiberglass directional arrows, the brochure really ought to show a detailed map, and doesn't. One brochure for the Tlaloc Trail, a 19-mile circuit intended for mountain bikes, depicts a vague rendering of the area. The Lincoln Horse Trail commences at the southeast corner of the parking lot, easing downward for one mile into the Bonito Valley as far east as the river, a good turnaround point for casual visitors. This horse path perseveres for 10 more miles. Carry a compass and canteen if you want to devote time to your explorations here.

In another mile down NM 214, look for the unexpectedly large complex of historic buildings at Fort Stanton (1855-1896). The fort was so designated to acknowledge Capt. H. Stanton, who was dispatched (like many of the soldiers here) by the Mescalero Apaches. Confederate forces briefly occupied the site in 1861, though later, union-sympathizer Kit Carson served as post commander for much of the Civil War. While the earliest structures have been destroyed, there are, in comparison to the vast majority of American frontier garrisons, several white-washed buildings in good condition dating to the late 1860s. Fort Stanton was one home of the black infantry troopers called Buffalo Soldiers by the Apaches. The outpost was touched by literary fame when Governor Lew Wallace wrote portions of the epic *Ben Hur* during his stay. The locale was run as a tubercular sanitarium after 1898, and then as a women's prison, and then as a public health hospital by the 1960s. A National Historic Landmark since 1966, the fort's status has been shaky recently and is currently in transition. Billy the Kid was once jailed in the building used as the dental clinic. Although not exactly open to the public in the usual sense, one can briefly walk the perimeter. Or, visit the museum, which operates on the grounds off a side road to the west. Keep your eyes peeled for the little sign.

In addition, the Rio Bonito Petroglyph Trail may be found approximately nine miles south of US 380 on NM 214. Watch for the brown sign on the west side of the road. You have to drive 2.2 more miles to the trailhead, moving towards Bonito Creek, which at this point wiggles off to the west. The trail is not difficult, but the problem with Rio Bonito is that the access route deteriorates quickly into a rocky track. Visitors in passenger cars should allow some extra time to foot-slog a serious portion of this stretch. The length of the actual hike equals 2.1 miles total. Located at its midpoint, handsome Petroglyph Rock was etched 1,000 years ago by the prehistoric aboriginals of southern New Mexico, in this case the Jornada branch of the Mogollon culture. Overall bracket dates for the pictographs span a couple of centuries in either direction. These fascinating images reveal sacred water deities (reminiscent of the Aztec god, Tlaloc), stylized bear paws, and war shields.

Back on NM 214, one hits the elegant Spence Theatre in another two miles (11 miles from US 380). It was designed by architect Antoine Predock of Albuquerque (call 336-4800 for tours). Built at a cost of $20 million, the structure's bold, soaring lines were fabricated in steel and encased by limestone imported from Spain. Behold the stepped waterfall and glass atrium. The 500-seat auditorium holds frequent performances.

North of Capitan, it's hard to ignore the Capitan Mountains, an isolated east-west mass (one of the few that doesn't go north-south) containing a big wilderness area. Spaniards explored and named the range during the 1700s. It's 23 miles long and only 8 miles wide. These uplands were the home of Smokey the Bear, found as a cub with burned feet clinging to a tree after a major forest fire that toasted 17,000 acres. The alpine summit, Capitan Peak, is 10,179 ft. high. It commands attention throughout a considerable region to the southeast. Yet the base of this igneous cordillera consists of upper Sonoran foothills, streaked with juniper, providing a contrast to the higher slopes. In cool weather, you can take a quiet spin through the lower elevations and scout for wild life in the early morning, saving the woods further up for when it's hot. From Capitan, Road C-1 runs to the north about two miles east of town. Sometimes called the Capitan Gap Road, sedans should be able to handle the first four or five miles. The route keeps going for a couple of more miles, now as F.R. 56, to Capitan Pass and the Summit Trail. This section can be hazardous after a rain, and extremely rough, so use your own judgment. You could simply trek part of the way to get some exercise.

Incidentally, if you head north from Capitan on NM 246, you'll curve around the north side of the Capitan Range. Some 32 miles from town, F.R. 130 splits off to the right (south) for a couple of miles, penetrating the mountains. This area is alleged to be the site of a UFO crash. Watch for a sign to Boy Scout Peak. F.R. 130 should be ok for regular automobiles and even involves one or two camping venues, but if you need more details, inquire at the Smokey Bear Station of the Lincoln National Forest.

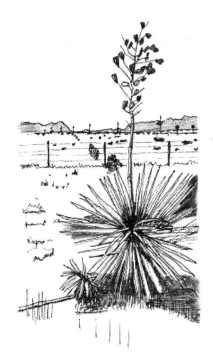

Sotol on Highway 360

Moreover, from US 380, the Salazar Canyon Road (also called C-2 or F.R. 57) will appear in approximately eight miles east of Capitan. It swerves northeast up to Baca Campground. F. R. 338, a rugged track, cuts off to the left a brief distance before the camping spot, a secondary route to Capitan Pass.

Small but pretty Lincoln rests twelve miles east of Capitan. The town, once 1000 strong but now down to 75 people, hangs daintily along Hwy. 380. Originally a Spanish farm community of the 1840s-50s, Lincoln boasts adobe and wood commercial buildings from the late nineteenth century, refurbished from the 1930s to the 1970s. Billy the Kid was tried here in the Lincoln County Courthouse, actually the old Murphy Store (ca. 1873), restored and open to the public. The Tundstall Store, likewise on the west side of town, is also open. The Wortley Hotel (653-4300) still functions as an inn with brass beds and meal service during the warm half of the year. County clerk Juan Patron's old shop—a single story adobe built around 1860 in the middle of town—is now a well-known B and B (653-4676; $80-120 range). The Ellis Country Inn, a Territorial period abode, sets the menu of Isaac's Table Restaurant on Wednesday-Saturday nights (by reservation only; open most of year). The Ellis takes overnight guests in its array of rooms and suites (east end; 653-4609; $70-110 range). Notice the reconstructed torreon along the main street. This medieval-looking stone tower, started in the 1800s, rebuilt in the 1900s, and recently covered with mud plaster, is similar to the ones colonials used for defending themselves during the seventeenth century. Additionally, the Lincoln County Historical Center has a fifteen-minute slide presentation explaining the village's violent past (closed Christmas, January 1, Easter, and Thanksgiving). Billy the Kid worked for John Tunstall, who was gunned down in 1878. Tunstall and L.G. Murphy were the main protagonists of the Lincoln County War, a conflict among competing ranchers for army beef contracts. Furthermore, Tunstall accused the local Sheriff, who was in Murphy's pocket, of misappropriating tax money. Billy (among his many colorful activities) resorted to taking out his boss's enemies after Tunstall was murdered, kicking off a year-long conflict. Billy escaped Lincoln after his arrest and confinement to be killed in 1881 by Sheriff Pat Garrett at Fort Sumner.

If you continue for some ten miles, one passes through the beautiful Hondo Valley and village of Hondo. Tinnie's Mecantile from the 1870s, now a restaurant, is maybe three miles more. Reversing direction by going west on Hwy. 70, the weekend traveler will chance upon an old school, church, post office, and polo ground of all things, at San Patricio. Billy the Kid hung out in the village of San Patricio, as did actress Helen Hayes. Artists John Meigs and Peter Hurd run galleries displaying their work (Meig's home is a gem if you can get inside). Actor Richard Farnsworth resided nearby until recently. Further along, the Museum of the American West (open daily 10-5; $6) at Ruidoso Downs examines the critical impact the horse had on frontier history, and Wild West fans will love the 12-passenger stagecoach from 1866. By the way, horse racing is big business in New Mexico. Ruidoso Downs (378-4431) is considered by many to be the state's most famous track, sponsoring thoroughbred races during the summer capped by the All-American Futurity at the end of the season on Labor Day. The purse for this competition between quarter horses exceeds two million dollars.

Truth or Consequences

Population: 7,200
Elevation: 4260 ft.
Distance from Albuquerque: 149 miles
Chamber of Commerce: 894-3536

The drive to Truth or Consequences on I –25 skips along to the west of the Rio Grande. South of Socorro, one traverses the gravel-terraced shoulders of the river, veneered by stone fragments that tumbled down mountain streams. This rigid landscape is defined by a variety of craggy forms, since both volcanic and fault block ranges convulse into view. The volcanic mountains tend to be on the right (west). The fault-blocked sierras are distinguishable by their multi-colored stripes, like a layer cake, derived from the deposition of contrasting materials during different epochs. Sedimentary layers cap the top. Many of these dry ranges are not high enough to support much vegetation. They jut boldly against the sky, brown and purple towers scratching hard against an unperturbed, spanking blue.

It seems strange that a warm, shallow sea covered southern New Mexico over 300 million years ago. Dinosaurs ruled the region eons later, their remains discovered within rock formations at Elephant Butte Reservoir. Today, New Mexico has the least surface water of almost any state, so regional lakes were created by damming up the Rio Grande as it slides down the Chihuahua Desert to the Gulf of Mexico. Irrigated lands below the main dam have absorbed the leftover salts once carried off by river currents. Worried environmentalists predict that someday these inviting waters will burst free of constraint.

Beyond the narrow precincts of the river, the surrounding deserts and mountains can seem forbidding. Nonetheless, many animals make their home here. Pronghorn antelope, oryx, javelina, bighorn sheep, deer, bear, cougar, and elk, and even occasional rare jaguar manage among varying habitats.

The Gila, a gigantic wilderness way to the west of Truth or Consequences, is of sufficient elevation to receive the moisture needed to nurture unencumbered forests. Though regulations are strict, Sierra County lures hunters throughout the fall and winter. Doves, quails, and pheasants are not uncommon. The weekend traveler may even hear the cawing of seagulls. These birds sometimes glide up the river corridor as far as Caballo and Elephant Butte Lakes, winging casually above the rocky terrain of cacti-studded campgrounds, unexpected visitors in a parched domain. They dine to some extent on grubs from fields stretching to Las Cruces. A few fortunate wayfarers also report seeing enormous pelicans in the area from time to time, an ancient species that recalls the evolutionary link of birds with Jurassic reptiles.

General

T or C, as it's called, is a retirement and recreational hub that takes advantage of the interstate trade. Government is a fairly big employer, but baby boomers escaping the angst of urban life are recent converts to the area along with some artists. These folks foresee revitalization and more tourism. Summer visitors come because of the propinquity to Elephant Butte Lake, the biggest reservoir in the state, attracting many sailors (there's a sailing club in New Mexico). The Memorial Day and July 4 weekends are busy. The hot springs were once enjoyed by the Apaches, and later by American soldiers of the 1800s who wanted to round them up. The dam eventually and completely inundated the old frontier garrison, Fort McRae, built around 1863. The soothing waters here continue to draw Albuquerqueans and "snowbirds" during the cold months in search of a steamy soak or massage at places with indoor facilities (the slightly alkaline water is 98-115 degrees). Winters, a tad milder in T or C than in Albuquerque, can be a good time for a quick getaway, since a few hostelries schedule lower rates during the slower time of year. T or C celebrates a Fiddlers Contest in April and/or October; a Fiesta plus Golf Tournament in May; and Geronimo Peace Days the second weekend in October. An annual car show takes place on Veteran's Day weekend in mid-November at the Veteran's Home (992 S. Broadway). This steadfast structure has served as a backdrop for at least one Rudolfo Anaya novel. For the last several years the car show has drawn 175 street rods and Edsels from California to Tennessee, a tribute to chrome as both an aesthetic and quasi-religious fetish.

By an odd quirk, the area of T or C was once known for a campsite named *Aleman*. The spot was situated just to the east during the colonial era, memorializing an infamous German trader of the late 1600s whose battered body was discovered in the desert. Then four families started the Spanish farming settlement of Las Palomas (the doves) seven miles to the south by the mid-nineteenth century. This romantic title, derived from the blissful avian inhabitants of local river cottonwoods, was swiped to designate the mineral waters upstream, where T or C stands. The Rio Grande originally coursed through a messy swamp that is today the main drag. The Ralph Edwards Park, presently at the foot of Broadway, lies along a remnant of stream frontage. Then cattle companies with exhausted workers "improved" the springs. The first housed bath dates to 1882. Cement tubs from this preliminary development used the flow of the Geronimo Spring as it percolated to the surface along the chief thoroughfare (the museum now sits adjacent). Sierra County was established in 1884. A few years later, shopkeepers like Otto Goetz decided to abbreviate and modernize Palomas Hot Springs into Hot Springs during the construction of Elephant Butte Dam in 1911-16. By the roaring 1920s, a health resort atmosphere had taken shape with the automobile. The cripple children's sanitarium, currently the Veteran's Center on a hill at the south edge of town, was one such project sponsored by Governor Tingley in 1937.

The handle Truth or Consequences came about when the city agreed to change its name once more to that of the Ralph Edwards radio and television show in 1950, when boosters figured the national exposure would jumpstart tourism. In recent times TV tycoon and environmentalist Ted Turner has purchased big hunks of property in the vicinity. Counting the Ladder Ranch near Hillsboro, Turner is the second largest private landowner in the state. Chile farming, under pressure from Mexican competitors, dominates the region further down towards Hatch. The annual chile harvest on Labor Day weekend (267-5050; 267-4489) ensnares 30,000 chile fanatics and features a parade plus a fiddling contest. Regional residents perceive NAFTA as an encouraging sign, in view of a proposed spaceport to the southeast of T or C.

Meanwhile downtown has been subject to a partial renovation. A handful of antique shops, bookstalls, health stores, and bait retailers add up to a lean but walkable city core.

Practicalities

Interstate exit 75 to the east cuts through the "suburb" of Williamsburg, and puts you on Broadway, the eventual location of a number of motels. Broadway soon splits into two branches. The northern branch becomes Main, a one-way heading west. In the meantime the southern branch of Broadway continues eastward. The two branches re-entwine, as they transform from east-west thoroughfares to a single north-south one, Date St., the address of yet more motels. Several establishments in the older portion of town, either right along Broadway or 1-2 blocks to the south, offer mineral baths. The rehabilitated 40s-era Charles Motel, on the left or north side of Broadway, has comfortable stove/frig accommodation at a reasonable price ($35-40 range; 601 Broadway; 894-7154). Private mineral hot baths (the water is 110 degrees) are $4. Massages start at $30. Look for pottery and specialty soaps in the lobby, or ask about reflexology treatments if you want to experience your feet from an enlightened perspective.

The funky Riverbend Hot Springs Lodge, with its multiple options and common kitchen, hangs near the southeast edge of town, a block south of Broadway ($35-50 range; 100 Austin Ave.; 894-6183). Mineral baths are free for guests. Note that address numbers get smaller as you move eastward. The Hay-Yo-Kay Hot Springs B and B (300 Austin; 894-2228), the oldest bathhouse in T or C, is closed Monday-Tuesday, but keeps five pools with gravel bottoms. Indian Hot Springs across the street maintains one large pool and modest lodging (218 Austin; 894-2018). The Artesian Baths (312 Marr; 894-2684) purvey private tubs and a small trailer court but no overnight guest rooms. The historical Marshall Hot Springs (311 Marr St.; two blocks south of Broadway) seems to be revamping its overnight facilities; baths cost $4 and massage services run at $28 for a half hour. An ambitious new addition behind City Hall between Main and Broadway, the swanky, peach-colored Sierra Grande Lodge and Spa employs a chef ($100-150 range; 501 McAdoo St.; 894-6976; 1-888-745-6343). Each room is dubbed for a legend of the Southwest, from Pancho Villa to Billy the Kid, the potential springboard for myriad fantasies. Inquire here about alternative therapies. Towards the north end of the city swinging back to the interstate, the Best Western Hot Springs Motor Inn ($60 range; heated pool; restaurant; takes pets; 2270 N. Date; 894-6665) can be reached quickly from exit 79. The Super 8 ($40-50 range; 2151 N.Date; 894-7888) is also at the north end, using exit 79 or driving up Date St. from downtown. The Holiday Inn sits in attendance next door advertising an inside pool ($60-70 range; 2251 N.Date; 283-2410). The Ace Lodge conveys a 60s look with its basic rooms and small pool located between the newer chains and in-town spots ($35-40 range; takes small pets; 1014 N. Date; 894-2151). Other motels crop up along Date St.

One also has the pleasing alternative of actually staying by the lake. To the north, cottontails hop around the grounds of the Quality Inn Elephant Butte Resort ($60-100 range depending on season; Hwy 195; 744-5431; continental breakfast) which has tennis courts, a golf course, pool, restaurant, and lounge. Take exit 83, veer left on NM 52, and go beneath the overpass to get onto NM 195. Go about 4 miles and watch for the signs. From the resort, Elephant Butte State Park is but two blocks away. The Marina Motel, between the Quality Inn and the park, manages suites with kitchenettes and utensils ($55-65 range; 744-5269). The directions are the same as for the resort, but look to the right (or south) side of 195 as you cruise down to the water. Last but not least, the Dam Site Recreation Area might be closer to the town's center, and this place is spiffing up its act with renovated cabins from the 1930s that nuzzle the lakeshore ($30-50 range, some w/kitchenette; 77B Engle Star Route; 894-2073). From Albuquerque, get off at exit 79 and proceed south along Date St. to the stoplight in T or C. Take a left onto 3rd St. A couple of day use areas line this route (NM 51). Keep going for 5 miles, headed east then north.

Incidentally, a couple of RV parks abide in town. Or, truck up NM 181 from Date St. to reach the state park and the resort community of Elephant Butte. RV campgrounds are proliferating on NM 181, such as the Center Court, while others, like the Cozy Cove (740-0745; full hook-ups; showers; laundromat), lie closer to the water on NM 195.

The scenic Dam Site Restaurant and Lounge has been a fixture here for some time grilling up seafood entrees. You can sip a cocktail on the patio, walk around the marina and little nature trails, or rent a pontoon to maneuver the calm water in case you don't own a boat. The restaurant usually opens 11-8, but may be dark Tues.-Thurs. in winter (that is, November-February; see directions above). Most other eateries are located pretty much along the main drag. Towards the south end, La Piñata (1990 S. Broadway) and the Hacienda (1615 S. Broadway) turn out New Mexican fare. The Stoplight Café, more or less in the middle at 280 N. Date, seems busy during breakfast and claims to serve Cajun food (go figure). Los Arcos (1400 N. Date; open for dinner) remains a standby for steaks, fish, and lobster, whereas the Chinese Lantern (414 Main St.) is another established choice. A few smaller cafes are also available, like the Hilltop across from the Ace Lodge (1301 N. Date). BBQ on Broadway (308 Broadway) and Town Talk (426 Broadway) anchor downtown. The Hot Springs Bakery (313 Broadway) appears to be the "in" spot for salads, rolls, and light entrees. At the north end, there are several options, including K-Bobs (2260 Date), which cooks up all three meals for a hungry clientele; the Santa Fe Diner operates across the street at the Holiday Inn. Pizza Hut (1934 N. Date), Subway (1900 N. Date), McDonalds, etc., also squat on this side of town. La Cocina generates a healthy trade from a hill overlooking the east side of Date. Meanwhile Hodges Restaurant (open 6:30 am-8 pm; Mondays 6:30 am-2 pm) will do you breakfast or a chicken bucket near the lake on Hwy. 195. If you want to go no frills/pack up the ice chest, T or C is big enough to have a major supermarket with a deli counter on the west side of Date. There are supply shops on route to the reservoir, such as Butte's General Store on NM 195, or Reel Fishing at 201 Canyon Rd. (turn just before the Quality Inn). Rocky's Lounge (315 Broadway), though sometimes closed for private parties, brings in entertainment during the weekend.

Things to do

The Geronimo Springs Museum (211 Main; open Mon.-Sat. 9-5; $2) is a nifty installation funded by the citizens of T or C. Four aging office buildings next to historic Geronimo Spring were converted into joint exhibition space. A vaguely Moorish, round arch design was added to the front. Governor Bruce King and Ralph Edwards were on hand for the opening in 1972. This place covers everything from mammoth skulls to lance points to local

Mimbres pottery to Apache artifacts. The Mimbres people were a subset of the more general Mogollon culture, the name given to south New Mexico's predecessors of contemporary Puebloans. The Mogollon left behind pithouse communities (dugout rooms with brush ceilings), above ground complexes of varying size, and lastly cliff dwellings, in the nearby valleys and forests of the Gila Wilderness. Mimbres Black-on-white pottery is justifiably respected, depicting stylized animals or exceptionally striking geometric designs. The Apaches arrived relatively late (1400s?), but they were eventually led by extraordinary figures such as Geronimo, Mangas Coloradas, Victorio, and Cochise. These names are still bandied about at dinnertime

Mimbres pottery design

by lodge owners enamored of the region's daring history. The Apaches harassed the Spaniards and then defied the American military, dominating the mountains to the west until almost the close of the nineteenth century. The theme of the Ralph Edwards Wing forms a contrasting note with its bizarre kitch from the TV program, as Edwards posed with many including Jayne Mansfield. Check out the colorful public art by Shel Neymark. The old spring now cascades down a mini-plaza sculpture consisting of fuchsia rocks, terracotta bunnies, and teeny mammoths.

The newer Callahans's Auto Museum (410 Cedar; open Mon-Sat. 9 am-5 pm; look for the sign on Date St.) showcases glossy vehicles from the 1920s to the 1960s. Steve McQueen owned the '51 Chrysler. Another cloudy day alternative is the Buffalo Bill Cactus Ranch (1600 S. Broadway; 894-0790; closed Mon.-Tues.). At the south end of town, this spot was opened originally by Seattle folks who, like some of their specimens, were transplants. There are a staggering number of cactus varieties, *many* more than most people realize, and this assortment derives from several continents. Leaves are the lilting luxury of plants that receive lots of water. Although the leafless cacti have adapted to dry conditions, many species develop an extremely specific range. Local heat-loving cacti put out blossoms in eye-popping scarlet and yellow during the hot months.

The big attraction here is Elephant Butte Lake, one of the top ten bass lakes in the nation. It's 40 miles long and has a surface area of 36,000 acres, a huge body of water by regional standards. It takes time for a newcomer to get used to a lake magically (and perhaps incongruously) mottling the beige and butterscotch desert. Once your eyes become adjusted, though, the area is not without a certain offhand appeal. Sunsets can pour a surreal look over the dry hills. The haphazard marina village fans out from NM 195 with a laid-back resort feeling, as it yawns within a sotol and cactus-covered wedge by the water.

About 700,000 to a million vacationers per year visit Elephant Butte State Park (744-5421), a going concern since 1984 encompassing a variety of campsites (RV, improved, and primitive). Park headquarters occupy a visitor center with exhibits near Lions Beach. From NM 195, simply pass the Quality Inn Resort, check in at the booth, and veer left onto Ridge Road. You'll run into a nice beach, maybe the only decent one in the state, within several blocks. One can also turn left from Ridge Road to encounter several camping circuits ($14), these winding around to Lions Beach from a slightly different angle. You can do a modicum of sunning, swimming, or Frisbee throwing here without necessarily karate chopping your neighbor. Primitive camping is allowed beyond the developed sites.

The reservoir has a long–but mostly inaccessible–shoreline, unless you possess a sailboat. However, the little playground on Ridge Road does contain a trailhead. Luchini Trail explores desert coves and gradually lumbers up to the Quality Inn after almost a mile. You can backtrack, although it's possible to keep going to reach the visitor center in order to make a complete loop. By the way, the concrete dam in the Dam Site Recreation Area definitely merits a nod. The dam is three miles south of the visitor center and beach. Follow the signs opposite the visitor center, or, take 3rd St. east from Date onto NM 51. At 306-feet high and 1,674-feet long, this dam was the

Elephant Butte & its lake

world's largest when built to facilitate irrigation agriculture all the way to Mexico. The "elephant's head" at the Dam Site Marina is really a volcanic plug, and interestingly, the jawbone of a prehistoric pachyderm was uncovered in the vicinity.

Caballo Lake State Park (743-3942), a birding area of sorts, lies 16 miles to the south. The reservoir drowned a portion of the original settlement of Las Palomas as of the 1930s. The park offers more RV and primitive camping, with a couple of sheltered picnic sites, against the tawny, arid background of the stark Caballo Mountains. *Caballo* means horse, a fanciful interpretation of the range's north end, reminiscent of a stallion's head. Century plants and beavertail cactus sculpt the campsites ($10-14) that are regularly invaded by roadrunners. New Mexico's third largest lake supports a tiny retirement community and post office. Concessionaires sell fishing supplies near the lake. The Caballo Café (open 8-3 and closed Mondays) operates at the entrance, a source of Sunday specials. Several RV parks flank NM 187, which extends south from the western portion of Broadway close to the interstate. You can also get to Caballo from exit 59. La Percha Dam State Park is four miles further, accessible via a unique timber bridge. There's a modern restroom with showers at the campsite and a hiking trail along the river. Anglers hang out around the dam, but picnickers enjoy a few tall trees and a lawn.

A wonderful ride from Truth or Consequences leads to the ghost towns of Chloride and Winston at the foot of the Black Range. You can get off I-25 at exit 83, but from town, head north on Date St. to hook up with NM 181. Some nine or so miles north of T or C, turn west on NM 52. Cuchillo is the first stop, 8 miles west of the interstate, named for the Apache chief Black Knife (*Cuchillo Negro*), as was the creek that watered the area. Cuchillo was a farming-trading entrepot from the 1880s-1920s. The Cuchillo Bar and Store dates to the middle 1800s and contains a gaggle of paraphernalia that evokes the old west. This establishment manages to perpetuate a brisk trade in cold beer. St. Joseph's Church was rebuilt in 1907, having been destroyed twice by floods. There's also a small museum. The Cuchillo Café (743-2591; Fri. 4-7; Sat. 12-7; Sun. 12-6) makes blue corn enchiladas and taquitos, which may be topped off with pecan treats concocted at a shop several doors down.

Winston (founded in 1881) appears 23 miles later as you approach the receding ridges of the Black Range, a sierra that runs north-south for almost 100 miles. Geronimo maintained hideouts within these peaks. Ranch live-stock including a couple of buffalo roam the terrain on route, browsing beneath the stippled shadows of rusting windmills. Frank Winston was a miner turned state senator whose home still exists on the western back street, accompanied by a school, carriage house, functioning bar, and Winston B and B (743-0208). Take a left at the Winston General Store to find the little bed and breakfast. It staffs a café everyday except Wednesday. Brick, adobe, and clapboard houses weather away softly next to grazing goats and horses. Chloride, 2.3 miles southwest of Winston (watch for the forest road to the left, past the general store), remains picturesque. There's been a degree of renovation in this otherwise isolated setting. The obvious main street con-tains a few atmospheric false-front stores. Within recent times some folks have even started a Pioneer Museum. The Pioneer Mercantile was last open in 1923, and this quaint, mostly log building held many of the town records as well as the original cash register, along with a number of bats.

Chloride shone as the center for silver chloride mining, which was kicked off in 1879 when an English teamster carrying freight tripped over the ore while trying frantically to hide from the Apaches. The Englishman survived. Other miners did not. Chloride used to buzz with 100 homes, militia headquarters, 3 general stores, 3 newspapers, bordellos, butcher shops, and

Buildings at Chloride

a candy store, before the Panic of 1893 squashed production. Thomas Edison once trudged up here to meet with resident Henry Schmidt concerning development of the state's first x-ray machine. You can walk up to the edge of the Gila National Forest that enshrouds the emerging mountains to the rear and picnic among the trees. Mining continues in this region, so don't be puzzled by occasional truck traffic.

Also to the west of T or C, an alternate route, NM 142, departs NM 52 after four miles (as measured from the interstate). You will stumble first into Placita, founded in 1840 by the Sedillo family. The San Lorenzo Church has been ministering here since 1919. Two miles down-road, at the end of 142 (18 miles west of I-25) stands Monticello, settled in 1856 around a partially surviving town square that once boasted a protective tower to warn of terrifying Apache raids. Originally called Cañada Alamosa, French postmaster Aristide Bourguet reconfigured the name in 1881 to recollect the Jefferson mansion. Monticello served as the headquarters of the Southern Apache Agency in the 1870s. Sections of the village's defensive walls are intact. Look for the cemetery (across the creek), irrigation ditch, old store, stage stop (now a private home), and church, first built in 1869 but reconstructed in 1908.

An arduous 200-mile state scenic byway, the Geronimo Trail (894-1968; 894-6600; 894-6677), circles through a few old mining hamlets, commemorating the legendary Chiricahua Apache war chief. Citizen groups have worked hard to formalize this particular backcountry route within the past several years. You should probably gas up in T or C, but if you forget, there ought to be a gas station open at either Hillsboro or San Lorenzo.

From T or C, head down 187 to 152, and then hang a right (west). The trace clips through Hillsboro and Kingston, tiny gems each peppered with historical buildings. In fact, the Black Range Mining District was organized in 1881. Hillsboro, the offspring of a gold rush, was briefly the seat of Sierra County. The Hillsboro General Store, 120 years old, whips up chocolate shakes, and a museum welcomes visitors on Main Street. One English lady (Sadie Orchard) ran a brothel here from the 1860s until well into the twentieth century. A smattering of adobe and masonry structures are now settling gracefully, although Hillsboro, not unlike Rip Van Winkle, really comes to life once each year, namely on Labor Day weekend with an Apple Festival. Nearby Kingston once sported 22 saloons, perhaps the largest silver boomtown in the state for few sensational moments. A church was built thanks to contributions from tipsy miners tossed into a hat one evening. The vacated Percha State Bank, and the rambling, stone-covered Black Range Lodge (currently a B and B; 895-5652), command appreciation even now just off the highway, about 8.5 miles west of Hillsboro, and to the right.

You squeeze through Emory Pass at 8,228 ft.. Take a right (northwest) at San Lorenzo onto NM 35. The Mimbres Valley, embracing the Mimbres River, was flourishing during the 1000s-1100s AD. Though local archeological sites are not as well preserved as the elaborate Anasazi villages of northern New Mexico, vibrant prehistoric communities grew crops and hunted the forests. The Mogollon people practiced inhumation (burials rather than cremation), and the impressive pottery interred with them often features a mysterious hole in the center. The Chiricahua Apache succeeded the ancients. These guerilla warriors in skirt flaps and buckskins were hopelessly in conflict with whites, whom they perceived as invading their territory. White settlers, subjected to incessant raids, could see the Apaches only as truculent savages. The Chiricahuas were once scattered into southeast Arizona, but many ultimately moved onto the Mescalero Apache Reservation in Ruidoso. Bear right at Forest Road 150, which weaves around the Continental Divide. Here you skim the edge of the nation's first official set-aside wilderness. The Gila was so designated in 1924. Ranchers and conservationists have been at serious odds with each other over the past decade concerning management priorities. The large numbers of elk and mule deer that live here are a real thrill for city-dwellers. Wolves have been reintroduced into these woodlands, in part to hold the elk population in check. Beware that this section is best handled by rugged vehicles and not recommended during winter, depending on snow. The 46-mile dirt road penetrates a couple of campgrounds and passes Wall Lake, a picnicking and fishing venue that's temporarily closed. From here, continue north to Beaverhead, and then right (east) on Rte. 59 to Winston, returning to T or C by way of NM 52.

To the east of T or C, pint-size Engle (ca. 1879) is some 17 miles away via NM 51. This out-of-the-way locale began life as a stage and railroad whistle stop, servicing the mines to the west. Later it housed workers of the Elephant Butte Dam project while contributing construction materials. The historical schoolhouse is still in use. Today, Engle focuses on the Chateau Sasennage and Duvallay vineyards (894-7244). Several wineries thrive in the southern portion of the state (at Tularosa, Mesilla, etc.), a reminder that viticulture cranked up in the Southwest early, during the 1600s at El Paso and at San Antonio south of Socorro. Engle's French-inspired vintages include both red and white wines; tasting room hours are variable.

Conchas Lake / Santa Rosa

Population of Conchas Lake: Seasonal, 200 or less
Elevation: 4320 ft.
Distance from Albuquerque: 159 miles
State Park Phone Numbers: 868-2270 (camping);
868-2988 (south lodge); 868-2251 (north end facilities)

The drive to Conchas Lake heads east along I-40 past Santa Rosa to Newkirk. Here one begins an encounter with the Great Plains, once the home of vast herds of buffalo, not to mention roaming bands of Comanche warriors that periodically mauled Albuquerque during the 1700s. This portion of the state is sparsely populated. Clines Corners is usually pretty busy, however, a rest stop for relentless busloads of heartland tourists in search of a thrifty meal or an exceptional collection of kitch from fudge to velvet paintings of Pancho Villa to rubber "Indian" artifacts. You can fuel up while perusing these giddy badges of American road travel.

Though mundane to some, the journey is not without stark beauty and color. Yellow prairie sunflowers dimple the sides of the highway during the hot months. Steep mesas erupt from the grassland. Capacious ranches are common. In addition to cows, denizens of the steppe are not difficult to spot, particularly if you depart the interstate for the lonely roads that zigzag off to the north and south connecting skimpy pockets of humanity. Hawks and enormous vultures occasionally come to rest on the tops of endless fence posts. I-40 retraces a portion of Route 66's later days, which can be experienced as the frontage road on the north side of the interstate at Cuervo, a railroad berg from the early 1900s. Here you'll find a gas station decorated with critter heads. A picturesque stone church stands on the south side, but not much else, since the four-lane literally swallowed up the town's residential mid-section. Meanwhile the region around Conchas Lake is drained by two major river systems. The Canadian River flows east to merge with the

Arkansas and the Mississippi, whereas the Pecos River runs south to splice into the Rio Grande. Coronado led his men southeast from Pecos Pueblo to explore the Rio Pecos as far as Santa Rosa in 1541. Francisco Chamuscado, another Spaniard, followed suit during the 1580s, gallivanting all the way to the Canadian River. Antonio Espejo-Beltrán, questing for minerals, reconnoitered the Pecos River Valley a year later before returning in disappointment to Mexico. Get off at exit 300 and truck north on NM 129, a cholla-specked scenic byway crossed by the old Goodnight cattle trail, which hiked from Texas through Fort Sumner, Pecos, or Las Vegas, to either Denver or Cheyenne at various times, where the animals fetched a good price. Trail bosses bemoaned the sizzling heat and suffocating dust of the drive. Thirsty steers often became crazed by whiffs of the Pecos River. Mesa Rica will greet the weekend traveler on the right, a limestone white and iron-red behemoth cresting 1000 ft. above the surrounding terrain.

General

Conchas Lake, if not exactly glamorous, is one of the more pleasing of New Mexico's reservoirs. Although only the state's fourth largest body of water at 10,000 acres, the lake is nicely nestled among several mesas, and it sprawls enough at 25 miles long (coupling the Canadian and Conchas Rivers) to invite a mild sense of expansiveness that lesser recreational lakes do not possess. Conchas was the state's biggest public works project during the Great Depression. Perhaps for this reason, the shoreline is softened here and there by mature trees, unlike other southwest lakes that can seem flopped down arbitrarily in raw settings without landscaping. Since there are few people other than weekenders, state workers, and retirees, there's abundant wildlife. Mountain lion tracks are discovered near the parking lot from time to time. Colonies of swallows buzz around the motel area. Geese tend to arrive in autumn.

This reservoir, a state park since 1955, has most of the amenities of a full-scale resort. A nine-hole grass golf course is situated at the south end, along with a decent lodge. The golf course makes for a fine walk when it's too chilly or too late in the day to tee off. Be absolutely certain it's empty before placing your skull on a collision course with golf ball. In addition, one will meet with a store, two restaurants, and year-round berths for hundreds of boats at two marinas. A second little store dwells on NM 104 just before the park entrance and sells petrol in addition to snacks. There are plenty of camping sites with full hookups, water, electricity, grills, and RV dump stations. Warm-water fishing is a biggie here, and the lake is well stocked with walleye and crappie.

Practicalities

Following NM 129 and then Rte.104 some 23 miles to the north of I-40, the weekend traveler should check in at the south end if you have motel reservations. The lodge is accessible from a turnoff to the left. There are two levels of accommodation. The less expensive rooms ($40 range) are in an older but fixed-up wing and offer one bed. The more expensive rooms ($70-80 range) are probably worth the cost because they contain two beds, while several of them front the water and/or have fireplaces. The couple of rooms at the terminus of this newer wing are larger and incorporate windows that frame the shore, affording a view of the fowl and small mammals that dart about the lake's edge during the early morning.

The south end also maintains a restaurant serving reasonably priced New Mexico dishes and gringo standards alongside picture windows. Ice is available on a limited basis. Camping facilities tickle this end on a rounded wedge of land outlined by the beginnings of a beach. Swimming from the rocks spilling below the lodge may be more appealing. The north end has a few cabins, a trailer park, dry boat storage, and the Conchas Café, cooking up mostly southwest fare plus prime rib on Saturdays. One can even rent a mobile home or a pontoon. The laid-back Tackle Box Lounge exists as the natural habitat of fishermen. Its outdoor tables aren't a bad hangout at sunset. Bands are frequently shipped in on Saturday evenings during summer. A shop stocks the requisite hats, bait, licenses, suntan oil, etc, but the grocery selection is minimal, so it's a good idea to tote your own goodies if you don't want to depend entirely on the two restaurants.

Things to do

If you don't own a boat for water skiing, the principal activity is to relax. Winter is cold, and the north end restaurant may be closed. Late spring and early fall are delightful for a quiet visit. Summers, and in particular Memorial

Day, July 4, and Labor Day, are crowded, though services are more in gear at this time. One can stroll all around the more developed spots and the network of side roads to boat ramps, a south end playground, etc., but there doesn't seem to be a lengthy trail system in

The spillway at the dam

place per se. The central recreation area next to the spillway sports a small beach with covered picnic tables, a location where the water is shallow for a generous distance (good for splashing vigorously). While primarily a flood control and fishing venue, Conchas Lake is clear enough to provide some ok swimming, wading, and sunbathing. Most of the 60-mile shoreline is private. Bring bug spray. Also, investigate the dam, authorized as an emergency relief project by President Roosevelt in 1935 thanks to the finagling of Governor Clyde Tingley. It's 1,250-feet long and 235-feet high. A breathtaking overlook gives you a fair sense of the landscape now inundated by water.

The Canadian River used to flood, devastating farming towns all the way to Oklahoma. A covey of administrative buildings have that unmistakable 1930s WPA feel. A nature trail works up to a petroglyph exhibited at the Corps of Engineers office by the dam's north edge. Shaded picnic tables can be found here as well. If you get restless, you can wander about the tiny resort community of Big Mesa that has sprung up west of the motel, a hodgepodge of comfortably settled trailers and summer homes guarded by plastic leprechauns. Scout the road to the left as you approach the lodge turnoff. From the north-end facilities, Bell Ranch Road turns into a partly unpaved stretch snaking north roughly a dozen miles to Bell Ranch. Originally the Montoya Land Grant from the 1820s, this place is presently a state historic site. The dairy, bunkhouses, and post office have disappeared, but a fine white house remains, once the property's headquarters.

The weekend traveler may wish to visit Santa Rosa, 114 miles from Albuquerque. Whether going to or coming from Conchas Lake, the town is handy for a meal or a quick overnight. Santa Rosa (population 2,500) is both small and unpretentious. It started off as a hacienda belonging to Don Celso Baca during the 1870s-80s. Railroad workers then descended on the area to lay track yoking the Rock Island Railroad to the Southern Pacific. In 1890 the growing village took its name from the now dilapidated adobe chapel constructed on the Baca ranch by 1879 (head down Third St. a.k.a. Rte. 91 for a mile, and look on the east side). This structure was deemed either for the first canonized saint of the New World (St. Rose of Lima), or for Don Celso's mother. St. Rose Parish was established in 1907. The mortuary bedecked by a porch across the street enfolds sections of the old Baca home. The city became a semi-important shipping point by the early 1900s, and businesses developed with the railroad. In the meantime a national highway system was proposed in 1922, assuming preliminary form some four years later. During the mid-1930s, Route 66 was reorganized. It took on an east-west alignment in Santa Rosa, and spawned over the next decade neon-lit cafes, motels (like the still-standing La Loma at 761 Route 66), and stream-line-moderne gas stations. Route 66 carried "Okies" fleeing the Dust Bowl as well as postwar migrants to California. John Ford shot a scene for the *Grapes of Wrath* here, including the snippet depicting Henry Fonda's passage under the train track at the Pecos River Bridge northwest of downtown. Later on, the interstate threatened to choke off Santa Rosa's linkage to long-distance travelers. Today, Santa Rosa depends on the ranching and farming trade. Nevertheless, national lodgings have taken a chance on the town, which is trying to grab more tourists.

Most of Santa Rosa's inns and cafes are strung along the easy-to-find main drag (Hwy. 84 blends into old Route 66 which doubles as Will Rogers Dr. and Parker Ave.). Get off I-40 at exit 275 or 277 and cruise for a couple of miles to select a stopover that appeals to you. Several chains are represented, though the mom-and-pop hostelries are usually more economical. The Tower (612 Route 66; $28-40 range) and the Sun & Sand (1120 Route 66) are two of the older entries on the south side of motel row near the teeny downtown. A second cluster of newer motels crops up a bit to the east. These include the Best Western Adobe Inn (1501 Will Rogers Dr.; $50-60 range; 472-3446), Days Inn (1830 Will Rogers Dr.; 472-5985), and the Ramada. Comfort Inn (3343 E. Will Rogers Dr.; $60 range; 472-5570; in-

Conchas Lake

door pool; takes pets for $10; a.m. rolls); Motel 6 (3400 E. Will Rogers Dr.; $40-50 range; 472-5923; small pets ok); and the Holiday Inn Express (3300 Will Rogers Dr.; $60 range; 472-5411; outdoor pool; a.m. bagels); constitute genial choices, among others, at the east end away from town. The Sundown RV Park (321 Route 66), Ramblin' Rose RV Park (602 Black Ave.; 472-3820), and Donnie's RV Park (2100 Route 66; 472-3942) cater to campers.

You'll pass four or five chain eateries on the chief thoroughfare, including Denny's, McDonalds, etc. The Silver Moon Café, from the 1950s on the east side, seems to be well liked by Pearl Bailey, Kareem el Jabar, and other notables. The attractive 30s-era Lake City Diner in a cleverly renovated bank (101 S. Fourth, downtown at corner of main street) is somewhat interesting. Joseph's Restaurant (865 Will Rogers Dr.; 472-3361), first opened as the Fiesta Drive-In during 1956, has become an institution in the middle of Santa Rosa. Its café and gift shop turn on the lights at 6 am. This place stays popular with tour buses that can pull up like giant whales spewing forth the bodies of hungry sightseers. Also, there's a deli at the intersection of Fourth St. and Corona, a block south of Route 66. Fourth St. was the center of the original business district, and a few turn-of-the-century buildings are holding on. The second version of the Guadalupe County Courthouse reposes here. The Comet II (217 W. Route 66; recommended; inexpensive to moderate) is a Route 66 relic a couple of blocks to the west of downtown, featuring simple beige booths along with a varied and above-average New Mexican menu. Some of the green chile comes from nearby Puerto de Luna, and the pies are a pleasant touch. Mateo's version of local cuisine (500 W. Route 66), a little further west, adds another alternative to the list.

There are several things to check out in Santa Rosa (Chamber of Commerce: 472-3763). First, auto fanatics will enjoy the new Route 66 Auto Museum (2766 Route 66; open daily; gift shop; snack bar; $5), which scratches the itch of one of America's favorite obsessions. Second, Blue Hole with its goldfish and 64 degree waters may be the best known attraction, an artesian spring 87-feet deep and 60-feet across, sustained by a crystalline, underground stream. Take 5th St. south from Will Rogers and then Lake Dr. to the east, past little Park Lake to Blue Hole Road. Scuba divers from Albuquerque to the Midwest train at this spot backed by sharp limestone.

Saturday mornings can bristle with activity; one needs a permit from the police department to dive. And third, Santa Rosa Lake, built for water storage of the Pecos River in 1980, lies seven miles north of town via an access road (from the main drag go north on Second St., east at the sign, then north). About 18,000 acres in size, Santa Rosa Lake State Park (472-3110) permits camping, windsurfing, and fishing. The Rocky Point Campground has 40 sites with hookups, water, flush toilets, showers, tables, and shelters. Juniper Park Campground is not as developed. There's a boat ramp for anglers in search of walleye pike or catfish. The drive over the dam forms a nifty diversion, while a visitor's center contains a display on the lake's fish stock. One or two trails braid around the reservoir through cholla cactus and juniper, the sign for a nature hike (.7 mile) popping up as you turn into the park grounds. The campsites could use more in the way of clever tree placements. Several low mesas knuckle up from the sandy-pink floor of high semi-desert and rolling plains, an amiably pretty if undramatic setting. Power Dam Lake and Perch Lake encircle Santa Rosa as well, available from the west side of NM 91 as it dips southward away from the city. Two miles south of town on River Road, the Rock Lake Hatchery rears walleye and trout. Watch for the sign on the western portion of Rte. 66.

History buffs will relish Puerto de Luna, Colonias, and Anton Chico. To get to Puerto de Luna, trek Third St. onto Route 91 (the Mesalands Scenic Byway) and continue south for ten miles. This unspoiled pilgrimage eases through the cliffs of a fertile, secluded canyon, blanketed with mesquite, juniper, sumac, and salt grass, fed by the Pecos River. One can always zero in on the waterway by observing the ribbon of cottonwoods. Puerto de Luna, founded in 1863 and briefly the largest outpost of the southeast New Mexico Territory, began life as the ranch of Melquiades Ramírez, who came here with six others to grow alfalfa and raise goats. José Luna from Los Lunas soon joined the group. Don José's house at an elevated pass (puerto) adjacent to the main road was dubbed Puerto de Luna. The village gained legitimacy by becoming the county seat in 1891, but Santa Rosa took over when it emerged as the local railroad center. The handsome Nuestra Señora de Refugio Church was constructed in 1882 and remodeled with a stone façade in 1921. It presides over one side of a grassy, informal open plaza. Opposite the post office sits an old saloon and store once frequented by Billy the Kid. The

San José Church at Colonias

original Guadalupe County Courthouse from the mid-1800s, meanwhile, endures in an abandoned field across from the church. Horses graze between green strips of priceless farmland interposed among squat, flat-topped red mesas. This place was used as a backdrop for Rudolfo Anaya's novel of the plains during the 1940s, *Bless me Ultima*. Though currently inhabited, Puerto de Luna feels lost to the modern world. A bridge at the far end of the village is encrusted with the nests of barn swallows that make rustling sounds against the cover of silence.

Tiny Colonias or Anton Chico can seem even more removed. Go maybe five miles west of Santa Rosa on the interstate, and turn north at the sign for Colonias. The 12-mile passable dirt road, a good route for spotting wildlife, leaves the twenty-first century behind. Colonias was a farming community that arose, like Puerto de Luna and Santa Rosa, to drink from the Pecos River during the 1800s, and today, it's tri-steepled San José Church is falling

Old Courthouse, Puerto de Luna

into ruin. Plans may be afoot to rehabilitate the landmark. There are few power lines, creating the impression of a pueblo tucked into a corner of Mexico rather than the United States. Sandstone markers reticulate a forlorn, atmospheric cemetery. Bison hunters called *ciboleros* lived here on and off from the 1830s, but then a modern exodus occurred as the Pecos River shifted course slightly. Last but not least, Anton Chico can be reached 35 miles northwest of Santa Rosa by taking Hwy. 84. Anton Chico has its roots in the 1820s with the gargantuan grant of the same title, given to Salvador Tapia. Drive 15 miles north of the interstate to Dilia, and west for 3-4 miles on NM 119. The St. Joseph Church in Lower Anton Chico was put up in 1857 with stained glass windows and other renovations from the 1920s. This settlement was the point of origin for the posse that captured Billy the Kid. Actually, *Upper* Anton Chico, just north of the main village on NM 386 below Tecolotito, is a tad older. Among the propped-up adobes and meandering acequias, notice the Blood of Christ Chapel, up an S-shaped hill. It was built in 1834, the site of Pat Garrett's wedding. A series of mesas surround you. These ranching locales from the nineteenth century will captivate weekend travelers yearning for an aftertaste of the old West.

Dulce / Chama

Population of Dulce: 3,500
Elevation: 7300 ft.
Distance from Albuquerque: 169 miles
Tribal offices: 759-3242

Dulce is the headquarters of the Jicarilla Apache Nation in New Mexico.
The trip to Dulce can be approached in several ways. One option is to go up
Hwy. 550 beyond Cuba, and then hang a right onto NM 537 at the Teepee
Rest Area. NM 537 is almost never crowded, *unless* you're going during a
festival. Yield to the impulse to tune in 660 AM on route to hear broadcasts
in native languages (primarily Navajo) or powwow music. Once in Dulce,
you are within easy striking distance of Chama (also covered below), should
you decide to engage in a little more tourist hubbub. The Jicarilla Reservation can be a restful weekend destination for those who are burned out on
the rat race and the more obvious choices. For one thing, it's large, now
totaling almost a million acres, thanks to a recent 100,000 acre-acquisition
of ranch lands bordering Heron Lake on the east side. In brief, the weekend
traveler will find some room to unwind. And since there are so few people,
this tranquil region still abounds in trophy elk, deer, and cougar, animals
that tend to move around. The elk climb or descend seasonally to various
altitudes in the perpetual quest for food, many animals venturing down from
Colorado during the winter. Horse Lake Mesa Park (some 14,000 acres) is
an elk preserve with a good-sized resident population, located a couple of
miles north of Stone Lake on J-8. Though this park is not a public facility in
the usual sense, the Game Department will allow people to look around if
you request permission courteously at the gate. If you have the time and a
very generous budget, reservation guides can even take you on a video safari
to tape mule deer buck during the rut in November-December (call the
Jicarilla Game and Fish Department for info: 759-3255 or 759-3442). Jodie

Foster and Carlos Santana, who take advantage of these services, are frequent guests.

The reservation straddles the Continental Divide, encompassing the foothills of the San Juan Mountains, and elevations here range from 6,500 to 10,200 ft.. Myriad birds, from eagles to turkeys to marsh waterfowl, stop or nest at several lakes, as well as the surrounding woodland. Also, some four thousand bears live in the state, a couple of these animals posing a recent problem in Dulce (stow trash carefully and be cautious about cooking outdoors, because bears have an acute sense of smell). While not the most dazzling landscape in New Mexico, the reservation does have profusely timbered mountains and canyons full of Ponderosa pine and scrub oak. The terrain graduates into sandstone bluffs, juniper-covered hills, flats, and sagebrush mesas towards the south end. The mustard-colored chamisa are large and fluffy after the monsoon rains. Snowfall can be heavy in winter, whereas July and August are typically the wettest months. A fire raged near Dulce a few years ago, but this section of forest has started to recover.

General

In general, the Apache, whose cultural characteristics can vary by geographic region, are descendants of the earlier Athabascans, who arrived from the far north through the Four Corners over seven centuries ago. The Apache were fierce marauders who created a great deal of havoc during the colonial era. The Jicarilla Apache, once nomadic, have lived near the New Mexico-Colorado border since at least the 1600s. The Apaches acquired horses from the Spaniards at this time, for which they exchanged animal skins from hunting expeditions carried out in both the mountains and the plains. By the turn of the eighteenth century, the colonists distinguished amongst the various Apache groups disbursed throughout the Southwest. The Jicarilla now resided along the eastern periphery of Puebloland. They spread out as far as Cimarron, and maybe even as far east as Kansas. These people traded at Taos and apparently began to learn farming from their Pueblo neighbors, becoming semisedentary. They were named Jicarilla because of their exceptional proficiency in basket making, and the baskets made into gourd-like drinking vessels achieved renown.

The Jicarilla Apache were dislodged during the 1700s because of intense Comanche raiding, which almost decimated New Mexico. The Jicarilla sought support from the Hispanos, thus turning momentarily into Spanish allies. When the Americans arrived, they bumped the Jicarilla off of prime hunting territory around Rayado, turning the area into ranches, and forcing the Jicarilla close to starvation. The military commenced to reservationize the Apache as of the 1870s, settling the Jicarilla to the west of Tierra Amarilla. President Grover Cleveland formally established the Jicarilla Reservation in 1887. The town of Dulce, meaning candy to commemorate the sweet water of a local spring, came into being. Wickiups, dwellings of slender poles covered with brush and grass, have long given way to modern homes and trailers, but a few houses may date to the first half of the 1900s. After a crushing bout with tuberculosis during the 1920s, the tribe began to administer its own affairs shortly before World War II. A little over a decade later, revenues and the birth rate gradually started to climb.

Today, ranch animals and timber sales supplement a comfortable income generated by tourism and expensive hunting excursions, plus substantial oil or gas leases. The Little Beaver Festival, held over a four day period the third weekend in July, is the busiest time, when the hotel may be booked as much as three to four months in advance. The fest promotes Apache culture with a vibrant powwow, parades, and a rodeo, tipped off by a grand entrance featuring participants in traditional dress. The sounds of drumming and singing fill the air, and visitors are welcome. The Gojiiya Celebration, a big reunion of two principal Jicarilla divisions scheduled for mid-September, takes place at Stone Lake. Native craft displays, races, and food booths complement costumed dancers (no cameras please, and they mean it). A Jicarilla Youth Fair occurs during the second week in June. Another powwow in mid-February celebrates the establishment of the reservation. You'll also find a small shopping center, grocery store, post office, modest gift shops, and gas stations at Dulce. Camping is available at several locales during the warm months ($5-10 fees are required).

Practicalities

Best Western operates a pretty good hotel in Dulce, the Jicarilla Inn (759-3663; about $70). There's an attractive restaurant and café here, along with a gift shop, lounge, and rental movie section. The El Ranchero Restaurant, currently open Monday through Friday, is located a mile east of Dulce.

Things to do

The reservation is dotted with a few pleasant lakes, although water levels can vary drastically, since these are mostly natural reservoirs fed by rain and winter snowmelt as opposed to dammed up rivers. When there has been a great deal of precipitation, one or two of these areas rank among the larger natural lakes in the state. Fishing licenses may be obtained from a variety of outlets including the Conoco at Dulce and Charlie's Sporting Goods in Albuquerque. It's a real good idea to call the Jicarilla Game Office (759-3255) for regulations and permits concerning hunting, fishing, camping, etc.

Dulce Lake is 70 acres in size, situated about five miles southwest of town on Hwy. 64. It has a launch ramp for boats and a few camping sites. Mundo Lake appears just over five miles south of Dulce via Road J-8. Mundo Lake, surrounded by low mountains and timber, is stocked with rainbow and brown trout. You can camp here as well, and there are a couple of tables, fire pits, and pit toilets. La Jara Lake, some 15 miles south of Dulce on Hwy. 537 and accessible by a short dirt road, provides camping opportunities also. La Jara Lake is small but pretty, and the south entrance off of eastbound J-15 (which reaches Stone Lake after eight miles) leads up to campsites near the forest. The unpaved access is heavily rutted, so make certain the roadbed is dry.

Enbom Lake comes up 12 miles south of Dulce along J-8 (the main paved route headed southward from the hotel area). Camping facilities include picnic tables and pit toilets. Horse Lake peeps into view not quite four miles to the east of Enbom on unpaved J-14. Weekend travelers are not allowed to camp or fish at this locale, but the marshy shore attracts certain types of avian visitors, such as yellow-headed blackbirds, ducks, etc.

Some 18 miles south of Dulce, Stone Lake can be reached via Road J-8. This particular setting may be the best known on the reservation because it is the site of the Gojiiya Ceremony in September. Falcons, vultures, and other birds make for interesting company, visible either overhead on near the water's edge. Although there isn't much shade, Stone Lake is the preferred venue for RV camping. If the main spots are crowded, another camping area exists along the southeastern shore, right over the spillway. Hayden

Lake, Stinking Lake, and Thompson Lake are clustered six to seven more miles to the south on J-8 and offer a joint camping site.

The Apache Nugget Casino is located off of US 64 on the west side of Dulce, several blocks behind the Cultural Center. You wouldn't think this unremarkable place would buzz, being removed from the Santa Fe or Albuquerque sphere, but it really cooks during certain times of the week and year. This facility seems to be open only rarely at present, though, as the tribal council decides to officially open a second, and yes, much bigger casino within the rest stop at the junction of NM 537 and Hwy. 550.

Cordova Canyon Ruins are accessible from the highway by going southeast on unpaved J-13. A few remains fleck the reservation, ranging from pithouses (600 AD) to escarpment shelters set up hundreds of years later. These settled remnants relate to the Anasazi, meaning either the arc of Chaco activities to the west, or a subgroup (the Gallina Culture) close to Cuba, or even Mesa Verde folk. The Apaches showed up too late, or led too mobile a lifestyle at this point, to leave much evidence of specific communities. If you're coming from town, take US 64 headed south, beyond Dulce Lake for a mile or two, and then go left on J-13 for roughly 9-10 miles. First check in at the Game Department (location described below) by leaving your name, since attitudes here concerning tourism fluctuate; let the field wardens know what you're up to. A map in the sportsman's brochure may be helpful. Note that J-13 should be monitored for drivability, especially after the rainy season.

The Arts and Crafts Museum (759-3242) perks along in a nondescript, greenish building on the north side of US 64. It's open 8:30 am-5 pm Monday to Friday and Saturday mornings. The exhibit gives one a chance to see both beadwork and baskets. Despite many obstacles, basketry is even now being produced in the Southwest, community elders occasionally passing the skills onto the next generation. Artisans often practice in the back room where they will answer questions. Different plants are required for this craft, the fibers allowed to age in a specific way. Willow, cattail, and cottonwood have been utilized for native basketry, and still are, but more obscure species are becoming harder to procure. Casual visitors can buy inexpensive bracelets, but don't be surprised by the larger baskets, some worth thousands of dollars. The prices of contemporary pieces are determined by several factors, including aesthetic appeal, fineness of weave, design complexity, materials, and relative scarcity.

The Cultural Center (759-1343) is another place that sometimes has info on Jicarilla doings. It's behind a picket fence on the west side of town where 64 bends abruptly to head east to Chama. One room is devoted to a small gift shop. The Jicarilla Game and Fish Department lies immediately to the west of the Cultural Center, where you can gather details concerning permits or critter activity.

The lovely Navajo River meanders just north of Dulce. Cruise up Hawk Drive (on the west side of the hotel) to a maintenance building, and then swing to the right over a hill onto J-2 for two miles. If you cross the waterway and keep going on J-2 a tad further, you'll discover picturesque spots for picnicking and wading surrounded by forested cliffs, mostly on the left. Walk down to this inviting stream and take off your shoes and socks. Blue and yellow flowers wave in the breeze throughout summer and early fall. You might want to hop over the Colorado border to reach microscopic Chromo, a few miles up Hwy. 84. Side roads from Chromo (try going east) crisscross verdant sheep ranches tucked between the peaks along or near the Navajo River.

Chama (population 1,200; elevation 7900 ft.) is squeezed beneath dizzying high altitude passes 25 miles to the east of Dulce on US 84/64. Chama lies at the intersection of the San Juan Mountains, and their southern arm called the Brazos Mountains, to the north and southeast, respectively. In the immediate area, Rabbit Peak (8641 ft.) hems Chama to the west, with Sugarloaf Mountain (10,525 ft.) to the east. The little valleys and rich summer pastures here have been appreciated during the historical era. Before Chama got going, the Tierra Amarilla Land Grant (1832) opened up a vast chunk of the regional landscape. Spin-off villages included Los Ojos and Brazos. In fact, protesters stormed the courthouse in Tierra Amarilla during an absolutely infamous episode of the 1960s to reclaim territory from neighboring land grants, resulting in both arrests and media hoopla. A few interesting if deteriorating buildings, mostly adobe but with Victorian mail-order trim, distinguish Tierra Amarilla.

Meanwhile Chama was itself becoming a sheep ranch by the 1870s as settlers edged even further north, and a boisterous railroad camp emerged a few years later. The Cumbres Pass route was selected after much debate to provide an outlet for the gold and silver riches gushing out of the San

Juan Range, and in 1880, the Denver and Rio Grande Railroad began construction of the San Juan extension through Chama, initiating the town's heyday. Saloons proliferated and did a thriving business. Nearby coal mines prospered. Many people cashed in through various methods, the notorious Charles Allison Gang regularly holding up the railroad. The sheep and timber industries also helped to sustain the area until the Depression. Then trucks began to displace the railroad. The once incredibly dense stands of timber had been overcut, and the town suffered reverses. The New Mexico Legislature bailed out the railroad line some years later, in 1970, as Chama began successfully to reshape its image into a tourist destination over the next two decades.

Summers are busy, but Chama is still unassuming compared to some of its upscale neighbors in Colorado. Rooms have become more expensive, however. There are a couple of "mini-malls" (Mountainview and Cumbres) with candy and gift shops designed to please visitors, though ranching is even now important to the surrounding region. Snow can blast this part of the state way into spring along lofty mountain passes, and the Chama Chile Ski Classic pulls in a crowd during February. Hail sometimes falls on exquisite, nearby alpine meadows in August. On the other hand, two state parks to the south attract boaters and campers. Chama has a music festival in July (756-2306), and offers deals on train tickets for students in May and June (756-2151).

Practicalities

The Branding Iron Restaurant (756-9195) is open for all three meals next to the motel of the same name. The Iron Skillet, opposite the depot, serves throughout the day until around 9 pm, the pots and pans staying hot from periodic fish frys. Viva Vera's (open 8 am to 8 pm everyday), on the east side of 84, has been popular since the 1960s for New Mexican cooking. The High Country Restaurant and Saloon is a favorite for steaks, burgers, and southwest plates, but may be closed in December. The Rendezvous, situated at the pass, gets cranked up at 5 pm. This place generates its own electricity to service hikers, snowmobilers, and other high altitude junkies. G's Café makes New Mexican specials, while Jennifer's Drive-Through can knock out a quickie breakfast, lunch, or dinner. Foster's Restaurant may be found within the neat historical hotel across from the train tracks. Other diners, a donut shop, and a pizza parlor complete Chama's list of eateries.

Chama proffers a gamut of alternatives for overnight stays. Terrace St. is opposite the train tracks and Maple St. lies a block more to the west. The purple-colored Parlor Car B and B (311 Terrace Ave; $50-90 range; 756-1946) is located right in the village of Chama. The Gandy Dancer B and B (299 Maple Ave. west of SR 17 via 3rd St.) operates from a residence built just before World War I, and rates vary seasonally ($65-110 range; 756-2191; lava lounge) with occasional specials. Cardin's Crossing B and B (551 Maple; $80 range; 756-2542) is run by artists who delight in period touches and homemade apple pie. Also right in town, the Lightheart Inn (756-2908) manages a smoke free environment of a couple of guest rooms and even advertises massages by appointment. The Casa de Martínez ($90-125 range; 588-7858) is another B and B, but this one bobs up in Los Ojos several miles to the south. In a handsome adobe house built during the 1850s when Los Ojos was founded, this place stays open February through October. Foster's (about $40) is a hotel from the 1880s, across the street from the railroad, and it has the added convenience of a restaurant serving all three meals and a bar. The rooms are claustrophobic but adequate with private baths. Foster's was a Harvey House facility at one point, and this structure represents one of the few to survive a fire that destroyed a portion of the historical area. The Branding Iron (756-2162; $70-80 range) is a big motel with comfortable accommodations on the west side of 84. The Chama Trails Inn ($50-60 range) keeps tidy little rooms close to the main intersection, whereas Cumbres Suites is yet another motel in the immediate vicinity of the village.

Other options stack up near the stream a short distance to the south. The Vista del Rio Lodge is on the highway's west side close to the village (756-218; $60-70 range). Look for the Little Creel Lodge (756-2382; $60-90 range), popular with anglers, on the west side of the highway as well, several blocks south of town. One can rent a small cabin, and a few come with kitchenettes and fireplaces. The Elkhorn Lodge (756-2105; $80-105 range) crops up further south right on the river, and this hostelry maintains rooms plus smallish cabins equipped with kitchens and utensils. The Lodge at Chama (756-2133; $225) is located off of a dirt road marked with a Chama Land and Cattle sign. This place is a swanky hunting lodge, and meals prepared by a chef are available during the heavily booked times of year. Oso Ranch (756-1876; $150-200 range), once owned by the Unser family, sits a few miles below Chama; take a left at the blue billboard. Corkin's Lodge (588-7261; east on 512 from US 84) is 16 miles southeast of Chama beneath the jagged cliffs of Los Brazos, and rates run from $140-165 for luxurious log cabins. The winter is slower, although a couple of units are kept open during the snow months to accommodate cross-country skiers. Rustic Stone House Lodge (588-7274; $60-250 range) hums along at Heron Lake with a variety of units that can sleep from two to eight people. The mid-sized stone house is private, positioned at an angle to the water, with wooden guest buildings arranged around the café and tiny store. You can contact guide services through the lodge to assist you in fishing-kayaking adventures. RV campers and squirrels have enjoyed this place for twenty years. Bring groceries.

Several of the lodges permit RV camping on their grounds, such as the new Sky Mountain Resort (south end of town; 756-1388) and the Little Creel Lodge. The Rio Chama RV Park (north end; 756-2303) caters to the recreational vehicle crowd as does the Twin Rivers Campground (near main intersection; 756-2218). Twin Rivers advertises showers, a laundromat, and a grocery store. The state parks also have facilities to accommodate RV campers along several loops next to the water; check out time is at 2 pm.

Things to do

The Cumbres and Toltec Railroad (1-888-286-2737) runs from May 26-October 21, connecting Chama with either Osier (the half-way point) or Antonito over some breathtaking terrain, including the Toltec Gorge. The train leaves at 10 am and returns 6 hours later from Osier. Overnight journeys to Antonito are likewise available that go back to Chama the following day. One can also grab an early bus (departing around 8 am) to Antonito in order to chug back to Chama on the train for a slightly different same-day outing. The depot is located on the east side of 84 (which becomes SR 17 headed north in town). You have to gasp at Cumbres Pass (elevation 10,015 ft.). Riding the rails behind an old steam engine is like capturing a glimpse of the Wild West, with a ghost town lunch attainable at Osier, where there's a restaurant and gift shop. One-day roundtrips on this narrow gauge should ring up to about $40 for adults and $20 for kids; if you wish to go all the way to Antonito (64 miles), it will cost $60 for adults and $40 for youngsters. Diverting at any time, the trip is especially scenic (and bustling) when the aspens start to shiver in irrepressible gold. Reservations are highly recommended, particularly on weekends. Special moonlight journeys are offered during Labor Day, and later in September, vintage freight cars are rounded up for photographers.

Trujillo Meadow may be reached by driving north on SR 17 for twelve miles, right over the Colorado border, and then west on well-graveled F.R. 118 for two miles. This high meadow is a beautiful space that fills up with outstanding wildflowers in summer, bisected by stands of forest. Bring your book to identify various species. You can camp here, or keep moving for two more miles to the fishing and birding reservoir. Trujillo Lake is a glorious locale nestled among Christmas-tree evergreens. Cross-country skiers trek these byways in winter.

The Ed Sargent Fish and Wildlife Area encompasses a 24,000-acre spread just north of Chama, established during the 1970s. From SR 17, turn left to zero in on Pine St. (two blocks west of the depot), and then follow Route 29 northward. This street becomes unpaved a few blocks past the laundromat and veers to the left. Road access is limited, but you can picnic here or fish for cutthroat trout. Camping is permitted at primitive sites near the entrance. Horseback riders frequent the refuge, which is actually managed from Santa Fe (827-7899). This environment furnishes a big time range for elk. You can park at the turnout before the corral, or ignore the sign, and drive down to the gate. To taste this region, walk for about fifteen minutes beyond the gate along the dirt roadway, over the narrow wood bridge to the rock cairn bearing a park plaque. A climb up the adjacent hill will afford you a superb view of lush fields and the surrounding mountains, a captivating sight for city-dwellers.

Brazos is a resort community 16 miles to the southeast of Chama. Go ten miles south of Chama, and then head east on 512 along the Rio Brazos. The deer come down from the cliffs and mountains in cold weather and early spring, and they can be fed by hand as they wander around.

Los Ojos

Los Ojos remains a nifty hamlet of historical adobes found 11 miles to the south of Chama and a half-mile from the highway. Tierra Wools (588-7231; open daily 9-6 in summer; 10-5 rest of year except Sundays) is a weaving studio that operates out of Los Ojos. The colorful gallery sells rugs, pillows, and big clumps of hand-dyed yarns that are spun from locally bred churro sheep. The cooperative uses outdoor dye pots set up over pinyon fires. This place, dedicated to preserving some of the old community-based livestock and textile traditions of New Mexico, runs both periodic classes and a guesthouse. You'll also see signs for the Parkview Fish Hatchery, open from 8-5. It's situated one mile further south along the village road.

Heron Lake State Park (588-7470) unfurls quite appealingly among Ponderosa pines at an altitude of 7186'. The hypnotic bluegreen waters here are designated as "quiet" (no loud motors), a good venue for sailing, windsurfing, canoeing and salmon fishing. Bald eagles winter at Heron, and mule deer occasionally dart around the picnic tables. Drive south of Chama for eleven miles, and then turn west immediately before Los Ojos, onto Hwy. 95. The visitor center should appear in about 7 miles. Several recreation areas including overlooks plus campsites ($6-14) line this route. Willow Creek pops up to the right shortly after the visitor building, with its RV and

Brazos Peak seen from the northeast corner of Heron Lake / "The Narrows"

tent slots tucked in among the trees. A nature trail winds down towards the shore. The turnoff to the Rio Chama Trail is located ten miles in. The hike starts from the carpark with a steep descent on a redwood staircase down to the Chama River, a fisherman's haven glinting in the sun. You can choose to continue over a wonderful suspension bridge, before trotting up to the top of a mesa, eventually reaching El Vado Lake in 5.5 miles. If you stay on Hwy. 95, several campsites beyond the dam flank small rocky beaches. Beyond this point, look for the west side site for primitive camping. Drinking water, flush toilets, utility hookups, a marina, boat ramps, and boat slips are all on the grounds of the park as well as a lodge and tiny café way to the rear.

Another state park, El Vado Lake (6900 ft.; 588-7247), holds 3200 surface acres of water, dating to the 1930s as a project to control spring runoff from the Chama River, after the local sawmill ran out of timber and sputtered to a halt. The dam is unique in that it has a steel face. The reservoir contains trout and salmon. Water skiing is popular in summer, while ice-fishing takes over winter. Go about twelve miles south of Chama, and hang a right (west) on NM 112 for some 14 miles. There are numerous improved campsites ($6-14), tables, grills, RV hookups, a grocery store, and summer café. The Lakeshore Inn maintains motel rooms.

Tres Ritos

Population: Seasonal, 100 or less
Elevation: 8500 ft.
Distance from Albuquerque: 173 miles via 518;
over 40 miles less via Highways 285, 76, 75

To get to Tres Ritos, take I-25 to Las Vegas, and then catch NM 518 past Storrie Lake State Park, a recreation area created just after World War I when the waters of the Gallinas River were dammed. (Note: if you are in a hurry, an approach from the west is quicker, but more congested, and duplicates the route used in another chapter). One then drives through Sapello. Sapello is renowned in archeological circles for its Paleoindian and Archaic sites, dating from eight to ten thousand years ago. Remarkable stone tools have been discovered from time to time that were used by prehistoric hunters to dispatch shaggy bison and other enormous animals. Hwy. 518 turns west at La Cueva, having abandoned glimpses of the sprawling open country below that marks the western boundary of the Great Plains. Regional villages came into being during the nineteenth century, as people dribbled over from valleys to the north of Santa Fe that had filled up during the 1700s. La Cueva (junction Route 442) was a supply ranch for Fort Union. The Victorian-era mill is still intact, once *the* place to meet for local get-togethers. The mill ran from 1870 until 1949. La Cueva boasts the old adobe home of prime mover Vicente Romero, plus the San Rafael Mission Church with its Gothic-style windows. The Salmon Raspberry Ranch, open summer through early fall, sells farm produce from sweet corn to garlic to pumpkins, not to mention flowers, sandwiches, and tamales. The raspberries may peak by late August. The road climbs into the forest as you draw near Mora, the county seat. Mora, established with a land grant in 1835, became the mercantile capital for the region, supporting stores, saloons, dance halls, and a lot of rowdy activity, including the occasional murder. A barrel of whiskey cost a reasonable $15. You can savor a taste of the town's history at the nearby Cleveland Mill Museum (ca.1900), but don't forget to enjoy the surrounding landscape. Although Precambrian rocks underlie the Mora Valley, huge boulders here may have been left behind by much more recent glaciers.

The Spanish Americans followed the Native Americans into this portion of the high country. Lots of wonderful stories have come from the depths of the Mora Valley depicting the lives of those who made a living within the folds of a rugged terrain. A recently published tale relates that an elderly villager with failing eyesight became lost here, but she felt safe upon noticing a furry but protective dog at her side. Terrified rescuers later informed her that the "dog" was in fact a bear. Abundant wildlife can still be found throughout the sparsely populated ranges of this region, occasionally creating real problems. The 9,000' Rincon Mountains soon arise to the right, sentinels marking the eastern slopes of the Sangre de Cristos. Winding creeks slide into view, including the Mora River, which bends north at Holman, and the Rio Pueblo, which skirts the highway. The mountainsides are painted in a dozen shades of green, and dense stands of fir trees billow "smoke" from air condensation. Don't be surprised if your ears pop.

General

A number of Hispano trappers worked this area before the inevitable farmers and ranchers arrived. The latter grew wheat among other things and kept sheep, goats, or cattle. Several groups of families moved into the Mora Valley, previously a stomping ground for the Comanche, as early as 1816. Mora (meaning blackberry) appears to have been either the surname of some key settlers, or a corruption of the French word for death, appropriate considering the swift demise of the pioneers from Indian raids and unfriendly animals. By the early 1900s, the economy picked up due to huge demands for lumber to supply railroad builders, eastern housing markets, and even the Panama Canal. Ambitious entrepreneurs purchased chunks of nearby land grants, setting up sawmills. Tres Ritos (named for the confluence of three streams: La Junta, El Pueblo, and Agua Piedra) was one place that took shape when the timber was stockpiled. Later, recreation was recognized as a potential mainstay. Since people doubted the practicality of skiing within a state as far south as New Mexico, most of the state's ski resorts are located at a base of 8000 ft. or above. Sipapu Lodge, at 8200 ft., nestles in this constricted valley but is sometimes listed under Vadito. Sipapu is one of the older resorts, dating to the 1950s. Nonetheless, the region as a whole has lost population, and frankly, sluggish development may be one reason why the area stays both beautiful and bucolic.

Magpies

Tres Ritos is a miniscule, sleepy mountain community that is best avoided in winter *unless* you are on the way to the ski lodge, as the snow pack here can be serious, starting roughly in November (plows are used regularly). Otherwise, summer is the best time, when the wildflowers reach their peak, trails and dirt roads are at their most accessible, and clear creeks gurgle over slippery rocks. Of course, the low-key atmosphere can be interrupted by the occasional howling of a disgruntled cow. Or elk. Mountain bluebirds fly amidst the forest branches like whirling, iridescent streaks of eye-grabbing color. Big black magpies with white stripes pause on fences. This area is an agreeable destination when you want to breath in some fresh air.

Practicalities

Restaurants in Tres Ritos are pretty much non-existent. There are a few eateries on the highway in Mora, including a pizza place, El Nicho Café, and Hatcha's Café. One can also chow down at Sipapu Lodge, which offers three meals a day and a bar open during the early evening, depending on demand. Picuris Pueblo maintains a café next to its gift shop that's about to reopen after some renovation. At this writing, a café (Teresa's) has popped up on Route 75 near the pueblo. Take along some groceries if you rent a cabin, because you won't run into supermarkets unless you decide to hit Taos.

The range of options for overnight stays is narrow, but the choices are not without interest. It's possible to camp in lovely La Junta and Durán Canyons; look for the brown sign on the north side of Hwy. 518. The weekend traveler will encounter a couple of formal camping areas. The Durán Canyon Campground (2 miles in) and La Junta Campground (4 miles in) usually cost $6, but one year went as high as $10. Primitive camping is allowed beyond the cattle guard, which is about 4.5 miles up the road. On busy summer weekends, however, campers squat at informal turnouts close to the highway. Forest Road 76 is an enticing route, and passenger cars can do some of it, but then the road deteriorates a bit further up. It's a good idea to have a high clearance vehicle in order to complete this 30-mile stretch to its terminus a few miles south of Angel Fire. The area is part of the gorgeous Carson National Forest (to discuss details, call 758-6200 for Taos office; 587-2255 for Peñasco office). Beware of setting up too close to the stream in case of truly bad weather. Other campsites crop up along Hwy. 518 as you head west.

Or, try a highway lodge. Tres Ritos Lodge ($40-70 range; 587-0486 or 587-2879) offers a variety of accommodation totaling 15 units, several containing fireplaces and/or right on a stream. Cabins come equipped with kitchens, baths, and utensils. RV parking costs $18 per night. There's a meeting room and a nice little store that sells fishing tackle. Walton's Lodge ($30-40 range; 587-2297) is a budget choice featuring kitchenettes with accessories, teeny fireplaces, and private baths. You can rent old movies from the office in case you get rained on during the afternoon (how do you think it stays so green up here anyway?). Walton's several cabins encircle a small, flowering driveway. Wood is $5 extra. Sipapu Lodge (587-2240; www.sipapunm.com) is fancier, with cozy rustic styling and a gamut of alternatives from rooms to suites. You can camp here ($8), or rent a bunk room with private bath and a hot plate ($30 range; bring your own linens). Cabins and small apartments ($50-60 range) have living rooms plus kitchenettes, whereas larger apartments or modified trailers ($70-80 range) supply the same or better amenities, but can sleep two to three times as many people. A few of these units are right on the road, so ask, should that make a difference. Additionally, sometimes a busload of visitors will barrel in from Santa Fe, overwhelming this place. It may be wise to book ahead of time. Sipapu advertises 15 ski runs from beginner to advanced. Obviously, these will be of little use to you in the summer. There is a volleyball net, on the other hand, not to mention a swimming-wading area in the Rio Pueblo and a fishing pond, while a trail exits from the rear of the property into the forest. Incidentally, a *sipapu* is a hole in the floor of a pueblo dwelling from which beings could emerge from the underworld.

Mora claims a very short list of motels. The Almanzar ($40 range; 387-5230) is two or three miles past Mora going west on NM 518. Look on the south side of the road and honk if nobody is in the office.

For a change of pace, check out the Star Hill Inn ($90 range; 425-5605; two-night minimum), a couple of dozen miles back in Sapello, one of a handful of astronomy retreats in the southwest. Star Hill Inn, written up in several magazines, maintains seven cottages perched among the pines, as well as an observatory, library, and rental telescopes. Inquire about their periodic workshops. Sapello is just a hiccup on the highway, and hence the skies are very dark at night. The owners will be happy to assist guests in celestial adventures.

Things to do

The weekend traveler will see the smallish sign for F.R. 76—Durán Canyon on the north side of Hwy. 518. This is a pretty locality, and Forest Road 76 snakes up the side of the Rio La Junta. Horses may be turned out to graze here in summer. A picnic can be fun, even if you do not have the equipment for an actual camping excursion. You'll spy at least one trail marker. Groves of trees vie with open areas as good spots, although the remote portion of the canyon may be more peaceful, and therefore more desirable, on a lively Saturday in July. Make sure the roadbed is dry if you're in a sedan.

There are also numerous hikes that literally come right down to Hwy. 518, so it's easy to pick one, park, and then follow the trail until you get ready to turn around. This is one region where you don't have to be clever or drive far to stumble over a trailhead. Serious hikers who intend long forays may wish to contact the Carson National Forest Offices.

One can take a side trip of a few minutes to Chacón. At Holman, truck north on NM 121 for seven miles. Holman Hill, a local landmark consisting of sandstone and shale, will be on your left (west), with the Rincon Mountains and the Mora River on your right side (east). This village became a stronghold of the Chacón family as of the 1880s with a small chapel dedicated to San Isidro. F.R. 138 and F.R. 17 digress a short way into the forest from the rear of Chacón, where you can stretch your legs. As you go back, reconnecting with NM 518, spend a moment at Holman, named for the postmaster Charles Holman. The old school and adobe church doze just off the road. During the 1970s miraculous holy images were glimpsed in the cracks of the church walls, galvanizing the avid attention of the media for a time.

Cleveland, like Holman, is often considered to be a spinoff of Mora. The Cleveland Roller Mill (387-2645; fee) is an interesting adobe building on the north side of 518 a couple of miles west of Mora (look for the sign and unpaved access road). The water-powered mill was in operation until the 1950s, when Mora's role as a regional breadbasket declined. The cast-iron rollers ground corn as well as wheat flour. The museum, some 4,000 square feet in size, usually opens during the weekends from 10-5, Memorial Day through October 31, though the hours can vary. The setting among the trees next to the proverbial babbling brook is worth the stop. By the way, the St. Vrain Mill, older by half a century, can be seen in Mora, a block or so up Route 434.

Morphy Lake State Park (elevation 7840 ft.; 387-2228) can be found to the southwest of Mora. Go south on Route 94 for four miles to Ledoux, and then follow the signs to the west for roughly 3.5 more miles. You will pass through remote valleys on F.R. 635. The last lap to this gleaming retreat (maybe .25 mile or less) is *extremely* rocky, but passenger cars with careful drivers can make it up the incline. Use your own judgment. Hauling a trailer up here may not be advisable, however. This scenic 30-acre lake amidst spruce and pine trees constitutes one of the few state parks that did not result from damming up a river. Removed, magical, and encircled by mountains, the lake is stocked with trout, and restricted boating (using oars or electric motors) is permitted. There are campsites ($8 for overnight) with pit toilets but no water facilities.

Picuris (population 375; 587-2519), 15 miles to the west of Tres Ritos, is New Mexico's most out-of-the-way pueblo. Prehistoric aboriginals dwelled in the surrounding region at least as early as 750 AD. Sometime between 1250 and 1300 AD, the Picuris Indians left a community called Pot Creek to establish their home in this secluded mountain vale. A striking and unusual aboveground ceremonial kiva, purportedly 700 years old, still stands, recall-

Morphy Lake State Park

ing the village's distant past. Sources disagree as to whether Picuris was visited by one of Coronado's men around 1540 or by Don Juan de Oñate in
1598. Fray Martin de Arvide set up San Lorenzo Mission during or before
1620-1625. Between two to three thousand individuals lived here at that
time. This building was smashed during the Pueblo Revolt, in which Picuris
residents played a significant part. For their role in the rebellion, the people
were taxed heavily, and many left. But by the mid-1700s, the village and a
renovated mission were successfully growing corn, wheat, and especially
effective herbs. Diseases and land grabs, however, continued to oppress Picuris,
whose doughty Tiwa-speaking populace remains small.

Nevertheless, a handsome adobe church was constructed in 1780, and
this edifice has been recently restored over a period of eight years. Contributions came from various parts of the United States and from neighboring
towns. A wall topped by a picturesque formal entryway surrounds the church.
These folks operate a little museum, gift shop, and two trout fishing lakes on
the reservation, also running the Hotel Santa Fe in Santa Fe. Picuris hosts
ceremonial dances on St. Anthony's Day, June 13. This group then celebrates San Lorenzo Day on August 10, when mass is followed by foot races,
afternoon dances, and pole climbs, and the public is welcome to attend but
no photographs are allowed.

Peñasco lies just to the southeast of Picuris Pueblo, and it may date to 1796. Several of the vintage adobes have been turned into summer properties. The local office of the Carson National Forest (587-2255) is situated here close to the highway, a source of maps and other info.

About 21 miles to the west of Tres Ritos, Las Trampas (the traps) is an alpine village with roots in a land grant issued in 1751. The allotment was bestowed upon twelve families. Community grants were given to groups of settlers during the colonial era to encourage development. By the 1800s, the villagers tried to move onto new parcels of arable land, starting more little towns, and in the ensuing years, much of the enormous grant was eventually lost. During the modern era, many trees were lost as well, because of the overexploitation of forested slopes for fuel. But this adobe berg can evoke the feeling of romantic New Mexico even now, and in fact, wooden plows were in use until only a couple of generations ago. The church was constructed during the 1760s, changing its name from Santo Tomás to San José de Gracia as of the 1880s. Repairs took place during the 1930s, including new bases for the towers. The structure was listed on the National Register by the 1970s. This is an exceptional building with walls some three to four feet thick. The Penitente Brotherhood once kept a death cart in this place carrying a carved skeleton draped in black. The church may be closed, but you can walk around the grounds and view the carved wood on the exterior, including the folk angel over the doorway, while an adjacent country store sells film, souvenirs, soda pop, etc.

Aztec

Population: 6,000
Elevation: 5644 ft.
Distance from Albuquerque: 179 miles
Chamber of Commerce: 334-9551

Hwy. 550 (old Route 44) winds northwest of Albuquerque, slicing transversely into the colorful, layer-cake rim of the Colorado Plateau and San Juan Basin. One crosses the Continental Divide at an island of forest a little beyond Cuba, just as the divide wrenches westward into Navajo country. Further along, the Counselor Trading Post has been on this route for not quite 70 years, carrying everything from cellophane cupcakes to traditional native rugs. At present, the store at Nageezi is closed. Nageezi means squash in Navajo, and many folks here still manage without running water. Careworn mirages within long vacant stretches, other trading posts at Blanco and Huerfano continue to sell Indian jewelry. Considered sacred by the Navajo, Huerfano Peak (7475 ft.) boils up to the east, its solitary position giving birth to the nickname of the Orphan, with sheer sides rising for 500 feet.

Glimpses of arid badlands tens of millions of years old erupt between clumps of juniper, chamisa, snakeweed, antelopebrush, and sunflowers. Oil and gas riches lie beneath these looming formations, gigantic pieces of rock candy crinkling along the roadway. You might see skipjacks, metal grasshoppers that bob up and down as they pump for oil. Bisti Oil Fields are located to the left several miles south of Farmington. At Bloomfield, the oil and gas wells give way to the valley of the San Juan River, itself a tributary of the Colorado. Meanwhile the Animas River cascades into Aztec from the icy lakes of the San Juan Mountains, sharp 14,000 foot spires piercing the northern horizon.

General

Having long filled up the areas alongside the Rio Grande and lower Chama River, farmers and a few trappers finally came to Aztec during the 1870s and 1880s. They were lured, like the Anasazi before them, by the production potential of valleys cradling the lower portions of mountain streams such as the Animas, La Plata, and San Juan Rivers. Settlers brought in a wheat threshing machine, and even set up a general store, and by 1890, the town was being formally laid out, appropriating its name from the acutely mislabeled ruins. Aztec soon became the seat of San Juan County and one of its principal trading centers. The place spawned a lot of wood and brick American Victoriana during the early 1900s. Hipped cottages emerged rather than the rounded adobe architecture of old neighborhoods in Santa Fe or Socorro. Several adobes were actually faced with brick later on. Industry blossomed when the Aztec Oil Syndicate cranked up during the 1920s, and in fact, Aztec was the first locale in the state to use natural gas in residential development.

By mid-century, Aztec's economy was being boosted by oil and gas production in a serious way. In the meantime the construction of Navajo Dam in 1963 further enhanced the flow of tourists, fishermen, hunters, and skiers into the vicinity. Aztec even earned an All-American City award for building a road to the dam without government aid. Nearby Bloomfield and Farmington, as well as Aztec, are benefiting from an upswing in retail trade and population, San Juan County accounting for a hefty percentage of New Mexico's growth since 1998. Major highways circling town roar with traffic. Other industries such as the motion picture business occasionally descend on the region to do location shoots, the most recent project being John Carpenter's *Ghosts of Mars*.

The green cottonwood bosques along the waterways of this region seem to be attracting new residents like a magnet, as well as weekend visitors in search of river recreation, ruins, and a small-town pace. The San Juan River rates as a top trout-fishing venue. The Animas River is the one that runs northeast-southwest through town. There's a little rose garden to one side of city hall (on N. Ash, a couple of blocks west of Main). A municipal park can be found on S. Light Plant Road, across the Animas and south from Aztec Blvd. (turn at Frontier Trophies). Pioneer Park on Main St., next to the museum, features a playground. Sporting good outlets, gift shops, and antique stores prosper within a small and walkable downtown. A special info center on Main Street is devoted to UFOs, Aztec being the site of several UFO conferences, and evidently, unusual visitations. Aztec's Fiesta Days in early July include a rodeo and a parade.

Practicalities

A portion of Main St. carries the Hwy. 550 sign as it runs south to north from Bloomfield up to Aztec Blvd. A busy thoroughfare, Aztec Blvd. is oriented east to west. It also bears the 550 designation for a few miles, until Hwy. 550 swerves north towards Colorado. Most restaurants are situated either on Main or Aztec Blvd. The popular Aztec Restaurant (107 Aztec Blvd.) makes down-home American and New Mexican specialties. The Las Palmas Café (603 Aztec Blvd.) serves all three meals, while the Highway Grill (401 N. Aztec), posed beneath the icon of an impaled Chrysler, dishes up roadhouse standards. With an influx of people into the Four Corners, fast food joints are sprouting like dandelions, and Sonic Drive-In, Blake's Lotaburger, A&W Drive-In, Wendy's, Pizza Hut, Subway, etc. are all represented. Oliver's is on the north side of Aztec Blvd., a couple of miles over the bridge to the west. The Atomic Expresso-Rio Grande Coffee Co. (122 N. Main, across from museum) opens its door until about 3 pm for gourmet caffeine, bakery items, light lunches, salads, etc. Also downtown, Rubio's (116 S. Main) appears to be the hot spot for Mexican food everyday except Monday, with patio seating in warm weather. Giovanni's, a lunchtime café, operates from Miss Gail's Inn on Main St.

Aztec doesn't rack up a huge roster of choices for lodging. Miss Gail's Inn (300 S. Main; $60-70 range; 334-3452) is a neat Victorian structure built in 1907, the area's first hotel, and the price includes breakfast. The Step Back Inn (103 W. Aztec; about $70; 334-1200) may be the town's fanciest hostelry, proffering a bit of historical atmosphere with rooms named for various pioneers, but positioned rather unromantically opposite the Safeway. The Enchantment Lodge (1800 W. Aztec; $45-50 range; 334-6143), a basic motel, bobs up on the west side of town. If these places don't appeal to you, one can find moderately priced motels in Bloomfield, though the highway is noisy. The Super 8 (US 64 at Hwy. 550 junction; $40-50 range; 632-

8886) takes pets for a $10 charge. Free coffee and rolls are available in the morning. The Bloomfield Motel (west on US 64 at 801 W. Broadway; $30 range; 632-3383) is a budget alternative that will also accommodate your critter unless he/she is particularly ferocious. Other possibilities crop up several miles to the west on US 64 (the Bloomfield Hwy.); look for the signs to the Motel 6, etc. Farmington, of course, has many motels, the chains typically offering a pool. The Chaco Inn (632-3646) keeps rooms at Nageezi. Going in the opposite direction, Abe's Motel ($50-60 range; some with kitchenettes; 632-2194) clocks in not quite five miles west of Navajo Dam on NM 173, in case you want to hang out near Navajo Lake, and these people also run a store and restaurant on the premises. The San Juan River Lodge (1796 Hwy. 173; $70 range; 632-1411) is another entry that throws in a continental breakfast.

By the way, the Ruins Rd. RV Park (334-3160; 312 Ruins Road) will be found in Aztec a few blocks south of Aztec Monument.

Things to do

It's fun to take a walk or drive around the historical section of Aztec. Inquire at the museum for the walking tour brochure, which costs a dollar. Though there are a few dwellings with a New Mexican flavor, most were influenced by European or eastern trends that became incorporated into American towns in a big way. Col. Williams's General Store (101 S. Main) is an adobe construction from 1890 that was covered with brick in 1919 when the building became a bank. The Waring Jewelry Store (103 S. Main, ca. 1910), Citizen's Bank Building (105 S. Main, ca. 1910), and Odd Fellow's Hall (107 S. Main, ca. 1903), as well as a dozen others, are further examples of Aztec's early days. Chaco St. seems to be the demarcation between streets marked either north or south. If you head east from Main one block to Church St., you'll encounter several residences worth a look. A few of the addresses on the 200 block of S. Church represent turn-of-the-century cottages. The Bailey House (201 S. Church) illustrates a simplified Queen Anne, a fancy asymmetrical style that often involved more than one texture. The Johnson House (at 116. S. Church; look to the back) is a surviving adobe from the 1870s. It was once a trading post. The Blitzke House (118 N. Church), a hipped cottage from 1910, symbolizes a housing type common throughout the West. (A hipped roof is one with four sides, rather than two, and the portion facing the street frequently contains a dormer). The Presbyterian Church (210 N. Church) was built of adobe block in 1889, and it functioned as a community meeting house for many years, with a parsonage at 119 N. Church constructed almost forty years later. One more block to the east, Fred Bunker built the Bunker-Beaver house (115 N. Mesa Verde), another Queen Anne, in 1907. The Green House (107 N. Mesa Verde), the home of Aztec's first mayor, is a very early small bungalow dating to about 1905. Bungalows were a simplified housing style with low roofs that became quite popular during the 1920s. The Eblen-Case House (ca. 1907) at 103 N. Mesa Verde exhibits exterior walls made from shingles and a charming octagonal tower. The Lobato House (109 S. Mesa Verde) is sometimes considered to be a Territorial style dwelling. The original lot was purchased in 1892 for twenty dollars. Mesa Verde St. is dotted with a number of structures from the early 1900s. The historical district reaches to the east for several blocks until you bump into the Lower Animas Irrigation Ditch, which runs to the south, serving the community of Aztec since the late 1870s.

The Aztec Museum and Pioneer Village (334-9829; 125 N. Main; open 9-5 in summer and 10-4 rest of year; closed Sundays) possess a hodgepodge of settler Americana. The museum was the old city hall back in the 1940s. You'll get a chance to ponder fossils, projectile points (that is, arrow heads) from nearby archeological sites, and a heavy dose of Victorian memorabilia. A cabin from the 1880s has been brought to the village section, along with a chapel (ca. 1906) and general store (ca. 1904) from nearby Cedar Hill. Founder's Day is celebrated at the museum on September 8 with craft demonstrations, parades, and a Wild West shoot-out. Docents wear period costumes as they wander around the milling crowd.

Aztec Ruins National Monument (334-6174; open 8 am-6 pm in summer and 9 am-5 pm rest of year; closed major holidays; $4) is located a couple of minutes off of Hwy. 550 as it heads west. Cross the river and take an immediate right onto Ruins Rd. Aztec Ruin was investigated during the 1870s and became a national monument by the 1920s, when major excavations peaked. It was listed as a World Heritage Site in 1987. This complex is a good example of an important Anasazi village of the Animas River region that was tied to the famous residential center at Chaco Canyon. In general, people who had made a living mostly from hunting and gathering concentrated into the San Juan Basin between 1000-1100 AD, becoming more dependent on agriculture. They probably counted on organized trade with their Chaco neighbors to get by. The whys and wherefores predisposing these apparent shifts—to a town, farming lifeway, and the subsequent abandonment of Aztec Ruin—have been hotly debated. The community started in earnest during the late 1000s and was occupied for a couple of hundred years. Some scholars argue that the inhabitants left this spot by the 1200s, to be replaced eventually by other folks from the Mesa Verde area to the north. Permanent desertion of the site occurred during the 1300s.

The .5-mile self-guided trail curls through West Ruin, a multi-story structure of about 400 rooms planned in the shape of an "E." Several rooms display intact original roofs, a real rarity. Walls of stone climb 30 feet high. The Great Kiva, reconstructed during the 1930s, is a round semi-subterranean ceremonial chamber, and though not ancient, it is certainly large (locals claim it's the biggest one anywhere). If you walk north, you trip into the Hubbard Site, a kiva that's considered to be unique (it has three concentric circular walls). In the meantime, East Ruin, the product of later residents, remains largely unexcavated. Exceptional artifacts including bone and wood tools, food remnants, jewelry, and even specks of clothing have been uncovered here. Take advantage of the 25-minute video presentation and gift shop.

It's entertaining to compare the Aztec Monument with Salmon Ruin. Salmon Ruin (632-2013; open 9-5 everyday and 12-5 on Sundays during winter; closed major holidays; $3) sits two or three miles west of Bloomfield on US 64, 20-30 minutes from Aztec. You'll see the signs on the highway. As you amble along the little trail, imagine the life of Peter Salmon, who homesteaded this property in the late nineteenth century. Salmon, the offspring of German immigrants, arrived from Indiana when barely out of his teens by way of Colorado. His son George took over the acreage involving the ruins. One wonders just how different this area was a thousand years ago. Archeologists figure that Salmon Ruin was a multi-component site, in other words, that there were distinct stages of building and major occupation. A big construction phase took place during the very tail end of the 1000s AD. Evidently Salmon Ruin was another chapter in Chaco's expansion, given the similarity of the sophisticated style of masonry and artifacts. Many of these spaces were plastered. There may have been around 110-150 ground floor rooms, whereas a second story of 50 more rooms was oriented east to west, once again arranged in a "C" or "E" shape. The whole complex seems pretty compact.

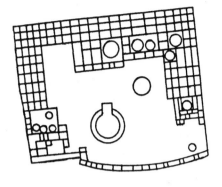

Diagram of the West Ruins / Aztec

Then another population moved in after a hiatus of some years, presumably from the Mesa Verde area, who added small circular kivas, while subdividing a few of the original chambers. This second residential sequence lasted for almost a century, until the late 1200s. Theories explaining the demise of the site invoke both the climate (severe drought) and the exhaustion of fragile, arable lands. While you're here, you might want to check out the San Juan County Archeological Research Center and Library, which has maintained a small museum with several exhibits since the 1970s. Included in the entry fee is Heritage Park. Hands-on displays encompass everything from Navajo hogans to Jicarilla Apache wickiups to George Salmon's rustic house.

Also west of Aztec is the B-Square Ranch/Bollack Museum (325-4275; 3901 Bloomfield Hwy.). This 12,000-acre refuge of fields and ponds is open 9-3 except Sundays and holidays. You have to call ahead of time to reserve a space on one of their free guided tours, which take place on the hour (last tour at 2 pm). The wildlife museum, the largest private one in the United States, contains some rare and endangered species gathered during ex-Governor Bollack's acquisitive prime. Go west on US 64 from Bloomfield, seven miles beyond Salmon Ruin, and as you approach Farmington, look for the intersection with Browning Pkwy., which barrels north. Keep driving west for 200 yards, where the weekend traveler will turn south in order to find the entrance gate. The property lies along the San Juan River and is managed by the Tom Bollack family.

Angel Peak (6989 ft.) flutters 22 miles south of Aztec or 15 miles south of Bloomfield off of Hwy. 550. This region is pleasant in spring or fall. Though there aren't many trees, oftentimes the Navajos will picnic here. Watch for the sign and veer east onto the unpaved road; picnic sites appear at the one mile and four mile point. You must continue over sagebrush flats edging Kutz Canyon to reach the campsite at the six mile point, run by the Bureau of Land Management (no water; 325-3581). An overlook from the campground provides the opportunity to contemplate a biblical-type barren wilderness of a few thousand acres. A nice hike starts at the northeast part of the camping circuit and tracks north for the first 500 feet to a ridge that slopes downward. From here, the path sticks to the ridge over rocky spots for slightly more than a mile. This moderately easy, but slippery, walk is a way to see the badlands close up. Once submerged under a shallow sea, layers of sandy mud were compacted into stone and then carved by both rain and wind. Drink in the pinkish, tan, lavender, and gray striations, noting the multiple little knobs of Angel Peak as they point skyward. Several formations are forty million years old. Snow-topped mountains 75 miles away manage to seem like a foamy ocean wave breaking over the surface of a far distant, dreamy background. You can return along the same route, or, follow the floor of the drainage upstream (eastward), along another ridge, climbing up through a notch to its crest. If you are confused by the side trails, go back the way you came. If one does the whole loop over the sandstone ledge (2.5 miles), the weekend traveler will wind up at a picnic shelter 100 yards from the point of origin. Allow maybe 1 and a half to a couple of hours. During the middle of summer, this place can be *really* hot, so carry a canteen.

The De-Na-Zin Wilderness, administered by the BLM (325-3581 in Farmington), sprawls 24 miles to the south of Bloomfield. The name derives from the Navajo word for cranes, these birds depicted in ancient petroglyphs found along the rim of the recreation zone. Many fossils have been uncovered within this region, once an inland ocean hundreds of millions of years ago, and later a swamp inhabited by dinosaurs some 70 million years ago. Small mammals live here now. You could see hawks or eagles scouting for them, while doves and pinyon jays are not unusual. You can get to the wilderness by heading west at the Christian Disciple Center onto unpaved County Road 7500 for 12 miles. It would not be wise to try this stretch

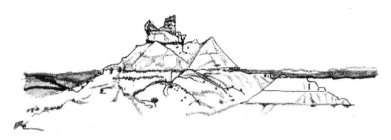

Angel Peak

during or right after bad weather. Landscape lovers will relish this vast open space of well over ten thousand acres, however, which unfolds as an eerie moonscape encompassing two important geological formations. The Fruitland Formation embraces interbedded sandstone, shale, mudstone, coal, and silt. Timeless gusts of air have eroded the soft sandstone into uncanny spikes. Kirtland Shale caps the mushroom-shaped landforms, revealing rocks of various colors and dominating the eastern portion of the wilderness. It's simple to undertake a hike along the washes, although there isn't much here in the way of formal trails per se. Try a picnic, or enjoy backpacking plus great photography at this locale, but don't collect anything, and definitely bring your own water and supplies.

Options for outdoor adventures

The Roy J. Retherford Wildlife Area has been owned by the Game and Fish Department (325-2101) for fifteen years. Take US 64 east of Bloomfield for roughly 3 miles, past the Blanco Blvd. sign. At an intersection, C.R. 4899 will point north, while C.R. 4901 cuts south to hook up with the San Juan River. Hang a right onto C.R. 4901, but take heed that this road has washed out once or twice after the summer monsoons. Locals use this 2.5-acre spot along the stream for catching trout and catfish. The waters here are warmer than at other locations closer to the dam, and can be less productive for that reason. Nonetheless, hawks frequent the vicinity, so birdwatchers should bring binoculars. Farmers have fenced around the public use area. No fires are allowed.

Another possibility is Largo Canyon. This isolated terrain makes for a Sunday excursion in clear, temperate weather. Cruise 10 miles east of Bloomfield (that is, one mile east of Blanco), on US 64. Blanco, incidentally, claims to be the oldest parish in the San Juan Basin, having recently celebrated its centennial with a fiesta. Unfortunately, the vintage church was destroyed by a flood, and a modern one now stands. Turn south onto washboardy C.R. 4450, where you should be able to see a sign for Cutter Dam. This drive allows one to rove the San Juan Basin Oilfield into some remote panoramas. The Cutter Dam Recreation Area, run by the Navajo and the BLM, shows up in 8.3 miles. The road to the dam will bend to the left, while a track to the right connects with Largo Canyon Rd. Unless you have a good map, a compass, and a high clearance car, it's probably safest to return the way you entered. Salt cedar and shrubs grow from the arroyos of desolate flats, as painted hillsides and sandstone cliffs hem the horizon. The Navajos have tenanted this region for many, many years, especially as a hunting and sheep penning reserve, and later, some plucky ranchers tried homesteading.

Other scenic alternatives link up to Hwy. 173, the eastern exit from Aztec. Though Utah's weird formations and pinnacles are better known, New Mexico has its share. Fantastic clumps of sandstone bump up in this direction. Note that these little access roads are sandy, and should only be attempted when dry (if you loose traction, remove the sand from around the tire while slipping small rocks under its front, so the rubber has something hard to grab). As one drives towards Navajo Lake, look for a turnoff to the south halfway between mileposts five and six. A well site should materialize in about a half-mile. From here, stop and get out, and scan the surroundings. Outcrop Arch ought to be visible 200 yards to the south, with Pillar Arch some 100 yards to the northeast. If you continue on NM 173, another dirt road treks northward right before (that is, west of) milepost 11. This road takes you into Horse Canyon. Curve left (northwest) at the first fork, which appears quickly. At the second fork, keep to the right for only a *very* short distance, until you can spy Peephole Arch over your right shoulder (that is, east). Peephole Arch speaks for itself, a squat oval of erosion within a giant, cream-toned hunk of rock. Someday the hole will wear and widen to the extent that the arch will eventually collapse.

Peephole Arch near Aztec

Simon Canyon, a pretty area, lies further away, and its access route meets the highway 18 miles east of Aztec via Hwy. 173. Look for the Simon Canyon sign, directing you northeast onto C.R. 4280 for a couple of miles. There's a big dip in the beginning, but the washboard itself isn't too bad. Simon Canyon is a steep-sided hideaway broken by numerous side canyons some 2 and 3/4 miles below Navajo Dam, a brief jog past Cottonwood Campground (a Navajo Lake State Park venue). The bottom is relatively flat. Streamlets here drain into the San Juan River, which has about a mile of frontage within the BLM property boundaries. Vegetation ranges from riverine trees along the flowing water at the base, to Douglas fir at the rims much higher up. Eagles have been spotted flying overhead in the cool months. Upkeep of the informal campsites could be better, though the BLM does not seem to have the wherewithal to manage everything within its princely domain. Simon Canyon can be a desirable getaway during early fall, when the cottonwoods transmute from green to shining gold to amber. The BLM may close off vehicle access eventually while maintaining this 3,000-acre preserve as a primitive hiking destination. Avoid the river trail during harsh rain because of potential flash floods.

Two dozen miles east of Aztec, Navajo Lake (632-2278) is a vast reservoir of 15,600 surface acres surrounded by pinyon pines and rambling low mesas at an elevation of 6085 ft.. This place is New Mexico's second largest state park. Jackrabbits plus gray-reddish deer mice zip around the campsites. The lake is fed primarily by winter snowmelt, and the shoreline meanders for 150 miles. The three principal camping areas are Pine (.5 miles north of the dam on NM 511), Sims Mesa (east of the dam via US 64 and NM 527), and Cottonwood-San Juan (the entrance five miles west of the dam from Hwy. 173 and C.R. 4280).

The Pine site is the most developed with full hookups, showers, park offices, and a nearby visitor center featuring displays. The campsites are perhaps too close together, but they are elevated, showing off a pleasing view of the water. Sims Mesa is harder to get to, while supplying some elbowroom, along with campsites, drinking water, restrooms, and a boat ramp. Anglers hankering after trout prefer the Cottonwood Campground, since the San Juan River is one of the best fishing spots in the West (call about restrictions). The recreation area spreads beneath the shading of riverside groves, containing an elevated platform (ok for wheelchairs) and a paved trail. You might catch sight of mallards, blue-winged teals, and mergansers. The dam itself, not quite a mile long, creates a spectacular overlook. The park's various amenities include boat slips, a dump station, a teeny playground, etc., attracting a half-million visitors annually. A small store and summertime café float next to the marina behind the visitor center. Mid-summer can be pretty warm, and winters chilly, so tent campers may not be comfortable except in late spring or early autumn. RV campers might enjoy this area at almost any time, as the lake remains open all year. June and July are the busiest months. Navajo Lake is stocked with brown trout, salmon, bluegill, channel catfish, and northern pike. The Sportsman Inn, a funky café, buzzes along four miles west of the dam, where you can buy lunch or gas.

Wherever you go—
always enjoy the road
"there & back again."

Colophon

Set in *Truesdell*,
designed by Frederic W. Goudy in 1931.
A classic oldstyle with a spry jaunt &
a congenial swash. It was given his
mother's maiden name.

•

designed by J. Bryan